THE INTERIOR DESIGN YEARBOOK 1989

THE INTERIOR DESIGN YEARBOOK 1989

General Editor Paul Atterbury

Weidenfeld and Nicolson, London
in association with

The Interior Design House Limited

TITLE PAGE *'Reveillon' from the Zoffany Archive Folio, attributed to the Reveillon Factory, c. 1785–8. (Also featured on pp. 6, 8, 20, 36, 40, 46, 52, 60, 72, 78, 92, 102.)*

RIGHT *Study by Christopher Nevile Design Partnership for The British Interior Design Exhibition 1988.*

First published in Great Britain in 1989 by
George Weidenfeld and Nicolson Limited
91 Clapham High Street, London SW4 7TA

Graphics by Robin Procter (Design Consultancy) Limited

Colour separations by Newsele Litho, Italy
Printed and bound by
Butler & Tanner Ltd, Frome and London

CONTENTS

Foreword

MARIO BUATTA

The rooms I always wanted to live in were out of the pages of English novels, magazines and the movies, filled with a rich variety of decorative objects, stacks of books, photographs, comfortable upholstered furniture, the walls and tabletops all covered with memorabilia – an expression of my lifelong ambition to rid myself of the remembrances of my *art moderne* past. Half my life later, I live in just that setting. I have screened out all those Thirties references and now live with secondhand objects from the eighteenth and nineteenth centuries, and I love it. It is a scrapbook of my life and it grows with every day.

My mother always said it was the spell my Aunt Mary cast over me. She was the original Auntie Mame, right out of the pages of Patrick Dennis. She lived in a way that was too olde worlde for my parents, but for me there was no other. Today we know it as the English country-house style, civilized and filled with creature comforts and things from the past, not exactly our past but providing links with ideas we have picked up along the way.

During the last twenty years the rarified John Fowler look has become the major influence for many young decorators across the United States. Finding one's own style in the world of decoration is not an easy job. In fact, it is confusing. Doing what you do best should be the goal. In the early 1960s I was influenced by the famous 'Buttah Yellow' room in Nancy Lancaster's London flat. John Fowler expressed everything that I loved about English houses – a wonderfully personal blend of the naive, sophistication, classicism, with a lot of wit thrown in for good measure. It was a recipe that I understood at once. I remember to this day the British *House and Garden Book of Decoration* I bought in 1962 and the discovery of my favourite room. At that time eclecticism had taken hold in the United States. English, French and Italian references were commonplace. Chintzes were seen but, in the words of the old adage about children, 'seldom heard'. In those days a chair or two in chintz was thought to be enough. I remember Billy Baldwin's recipe for a contemporary room: 'just three chairs in this chintz, trés chic, yes!' He was a master of the understated look and his rooms still look undated and fresh. A visit to England in 1961 proved that the country-house look was the love of my life. Two years later I returned, determined to meet John Fowler and Nancy Lancaster, and I did. John was a wonderful teacher and Mrs Lancaster a great student. Often roles were reversed as they combined the best of English and American decoration into a formula which is still unchallenged. This was the turning point of my career.

In 1969 I used the style in my first show-house room and my colleagues looked on in amazement and giggled at the bows and fabrics adorning my pictures and mirrors, my ruffled pillow cases, my curtain edgings and chintz piled upon chintz. Was I mad? I seemed to be, but the magazines wanted more, saying it was what we should be looking for. *The New York Times* featured the room in colour under the heading 'English Style – the new direction in design'. In the ensuing years more showhouse rooms confirmed the style and then in the 1980s, with people looking for ways to express their new wealth, Colefax and Fowler became the password in decorating circles. The new generation of decorating girls were ruffling every curtain and pillow in sight. The element of restraint, which was after all what John Fowler and Nancy Lancaster were all about, was quickly lost. Shops selling the eighteenth-century look sprang up all around New York and its outlying suburbs. In one section of New York today there are no less than twelve shops within three blocks devoted to the English country style. Style handbooks appeared everywhere, with plenty of chintz recipes for the tired eclectic. Antique shops sold more twisted candlesticks, ivory and horn handled magnifying glasses and Staffordshire china than can ever have existed in the nineteenth century. Today magazines continue to promote the style with interiors filled with chintz, and the old pro decorators have simply added 'English country' to the eclectic range of styles on offer. Everyone unhappy with their decoration thinks that a little chintz might warm up their uncozy rooms, and who am I to say no? In the last three years I have entered the chintz business myself, and have been hailed the Prince of Chintz.

As the excesses of the Reagan era end, there are signs of a new conservatism calling for a return to Neo-classicism. Over the fourteen years that I have chaired the New York winter antiques show, the floor has filled with more and more English antiques, and in January 1989 there was not an English dealer worth his Dover sole who did not respond to the call from the other side of the Atlantic for the finest Neo-classical antiquities. This is not to say that all those ruffled chintz ladies are about to lose their ropes and tassels, for the new ingredients will simply be found space in their Anglicized interiors.

Who is to say that English country style is not here to stay? After all, it was the eccentrics of the British Isles and their colours that started American style in the first place. We were English in the first place, and in many ways we still are. Long live civilized England.

Mario Buatta

MARIO BUATTA, New York, 1989

The British Interior Design Exhibition: Review 1988

STEPHEN CALLOWAY

Entrance arch to the 1988 British Interior Design Exhibition by Richard Lowe.

*T*he wonderful thing about design exhibitions in general, and interior design shows in particular, is that they tell us so much about ourselves and about what Trollope called 'The Way We Live Now'. Ever since the Great Exhibition of 1851 brought the 'Arts and Manufactures of all Nations' to Hyde Park, professional designers, design pundits and an often well-informed general public have seen exhibitions as the forum in which current styles and new ideas are weighed against traditional materials and methods at a national or international level. In the latter part of the nineteenth century the great European exhibitions tended increasingly to focus on the decorative arts. The culmination of this trend can be seen in the extraordinary *Exposition des Arts Décoratifs* staged in Paris in 1925, which so crystalized the style of the moment that it gave us the name Art Deco.

By the Thirties smaller shows devoted both to avantgarde and more traditional decoration had become an important feature of the scene, with the larger firms competing to show the most elaborate and luxurious room settings. Decorators such as the grand Paris and New York firm, Alavoine, had always realized the potential of the room set as a way of directing public attention to their taste and skills. As early as 1893, at the Chicago Columbian Exposition, they had shown a 'Marie Antoinette Room', a clever blend of the old and the new in

Dining Room by Simon Playle.

Morning Room by Joanna Trading.

which genuine period pieces and decorative details were thrown together with an unmistakably fin-de-siècle opulence.

In more recent years design and decoration exhibitions have shown a welcome tendency to move away from the product-oriented, suburban and sub-modern world of the post-war trade fairs. In New York the celebrated Kip's Bay Show House led the way by gathering some of America's leading exponents of grand, traditional decoration and, letting each of them loose on a different room of the house, created a show-case of contemporary decoration far more in touch, it has been argued,

RIGHT *Study by Alidad.*

Hallway by Parish-Hadley.

with the way in which most people would like to live. In England there have been a number of similar experiments which have drawn on the talents of a wide range of designers from both the mainstream and the more subversive fringes of the design world. In the latter category the House of Beauty and Culture broke some interesting new ground in its choice of material and manner of presentation, whilst The British Interior Design Exhibition (1982), in a Nash house in Regent's Park decorated by a number of leading British decorators and firms, followed the Kip's Bay model more closely by presenting a conspectus of basically traditional approaches to the enrichment of a fine London town-house. The direct successor to this presentation was The British Interior Design

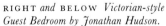

ABOVE *Master Bedroom by Anna Tatham with fabrics by Thorp & May Designs.*

RIGHT *and* BELOW *Victorian-style Guest Bedroom by Jonathan Hudson.*

Exhibition (1988), again organized by Fleur Rossdale, in which more than twenty designers created elaborate rooms within a purpose-built labyrinthine setting in the town hall in Chelsea, one of the heartlands of High Style decoration in England.

Perhaps the most instantly striking aspect of the room settings on display at the Chelsea show was the degree to which 'period style' predominated over 'modern' approaches to the creation of decorative schemes for the domestic interior of today. If the show was representative of the current attitudes and trends in British design and decoration, and it seems fair to say that it was, then future historians of taste will find in the exhibition not merely a record of 'the way we live now' but also a revelation of a generation that is

ABOVE *Nursery by Rossie Designs.*

LEFT *Bedroom with furniture by Sudeley Design.*

BELOW *Ante-Room by Ian Shaw.*

Kitchen by Blase Designs, a room in which to cook, eat, entertain and work.

obsessed with the past, or at least with its decorative legacies.

Charles McCorquodale wrote in his introductory remarks to the exhibition catalogue that much of the work on show could be seen as a 'consolidation of the romantic trends of the last two decades.' This is undoubtedly true, and yet what we are watching is the unfolding of a much more recent shift in popular taste; a move by an ever-increasing section of the population away from contemporary styling and towards the sort of eclectic, historically allusive decoration that had previously been the cult interest of a small minority of taste-makers. Where once decorators like John Fowler or Geoffrey Bennison worked for a tiny circle of sympathetic clients, now the larger firms and even High Street furnishing shops encourage the taste for a largely fictionalized English Country House look.

The enormous and worldwide acceptance of the English Country House look makes a

Dining Room by Rory Ramsden in full chromatic colour with dramatic lighting effects.

Boardroom by Beckett & Graham with furniture by David Linley.

fascinating study. As one of the most intriguing consequences (along with the post-modern movements in architecture) of the crisis of confidence in the International Modern aesthetic, it has without doubt proved one of the most potent influences in the development of the vocabulary of decoration in the last ten years. The more cynical observer will point to this obsession with the styles of the past and characterize the Eighties as years of living not dangerously, but comfortably; as a period in which the New Right have a little too conspicuously laundered New Money into some slightly imperfect version of the trappings with which Old Money once insulated itself from reality. This 'Upstairs Downstairs' aspect of the revival of interest in period detail and styles is however only a small part of the return to a richer, more historically and visually literate perspective; at last, an unashamedly eclectic view of the ways in which decoration can express not only our social but our cultural aspirations.

ABOVE *Breakfast Room by Indiaworks.*

BELOW *Chairman's Office by Gordon Lindsay.*

Library by Woodstock Designs with fabrics by Spencer-Churchill Designs.

There are many who seek the reassurance that a good scheme of decoration can bring. But at the same time it is well to remember that the arrangement and ornamentation of the spaces in which we live, and the disposition of our personal possessions in those rooms, has become in the late twentieth century perhaps the only art which remains universally practised.

It is an attitude echoed by that doyen of the English and international decoration scene, David Hicks, who wrote: 'Good design must work for the people who will use it. The best rooms have something to say about the people who live in them. Their story can be told in colour, shape, texture and pattern.' This excellent maxim, fruit of thirty years in the thoughtful yet bold pursuit of excellence in the profession, was admirably illustrated in the Hicks room in the 1988 show, an impressive scheme in which the designer and his team created a stylish, formal arrangement of several specially designed pieces. Here the effect, as in all the best David Hicks rooms, was of precise graphic clarity and of freshness informed by an intense love for, and knowledge of, the forms of the past.

These qualities characterized another popular exhibit, a bathroom of almost Soanian complexity carried

out in the pale tonalities and blond woods of northern Biedermeier by Anthony Paine Ltd. By contrast, many of the other successful schemes with a distinct period flavour adopted a richer, darker palette which has come to be used for rooms other than those in which to dine.

Geoffrey Bennison's successors in the Pimlico Road excel at this grandly scaled, opulent look in which monumental pieces of furniture are played off against the intricate patterns of document fabrics, but memorable schemes in a not dissimilar vein were assembled

Bathroom, designed by Anthony Paine and built by Wiltshier Interiors.

LEFT *Sitting Room by David Hicks International.*

RIGHT *Drawing Room by Bennison.*

LEFT *and* ABOVE *Abstract Space by Mercier – London.*

RIGHT *Entrance by Parke Interiors and Machin Designs.*

by several other firms including Norland Interiors. Their fine group of well-chosen pieces of gothick furniture made a deliciously associative study, redolent if not exactly of Horace Walpole, then perhaps of Bulwer Lytton or Sir Walter Scott.

The general reliance on the delightful patterns of old English chintzes and the good colouring of document wallpapers coupled with safe brown wood or painted furniture of the Regency period made the efforts of those who had contrived something deliberately different all the more refreshing. The London-based Mercier partnership showed a space in which unusual materials such as distressed copper mouldings combined with rich dark natural stone flooring and darkened lookingglass to create a 'poetical' setting for works of art including a new chandelier of jagged metal and a fine old bronze *putto*.

The most confident and telling use of recent objects was made by Christopher Nevile, whose study room set was a subtle play on grand palazzo style, achieved by the choice of pieces by contemporary designer-craftsmen working in a bold, neo-baroque or neoclassical idiom. Marbling, stone effects and grandly grained double doors set the scene, with a fine and colourful inlaid linoleum floor by Jenny Moncur underscoring the theme.

BELOW *Gothic-style Sitting Room by Norland Interiors.*

Objects included bizarre pieces by Mark Brazier-Jones in welded metal enriched with glass lenses, and painted silk panels by Carolyn Quartermaine.

In many ways this room by Christopher Nevile may be seen to represent the most appealing, innovative vein of British design today. There can be no doubt that with an ever wider dissemination of the English Country House look it will rapidly begin to loose its cachet, and as the supplies of good antique furnishings, pictures and other decorative objects gradually run dry we shall have to look to the desig-ner-makers of new things. Now, then, is the moment to seize the opportunity to measure ourselves against the achievements of the past. Certainly we should value and preserve the past, but equally we should, as our ancestors did, go out and commission the best that we can afford from contemporary craftsmen. Now is the moment when we need to begin to re-furnish our Palace of Art, mixing the best of the old with the best of the new. Now is the moment when we should be making a confident statement of our own taste; a statement informed by our love of the past, but one wholly of today.

Contributors to the British Interior Design Exhibition 1988:

PARKE INTERIORS LTD

MACHIN DESIGNS LTD

DAVID HICKS INTERNATIONAL

NORLAND INTERIORS

BLASE DESIGNS PLC

BENNISON

RORY RAMSDEN LTD

WOODSTOCK DESIGNS

SPENCER-CHURCHILL DESIGNS LTD

GORDON LINDSAY

MERCIER – LONDON

ANNA TATHAM

THORP & MAY DESIGNS LTD

ANTHONY PAINE LTD

WILTSHIER INTERIORS LTD

ALIDAD LTD

BECKETT & GRAHAM LTD

JONATHAN HUDSON INTERIOR DECORATIONS

INDIAWORKS

SUDELEY DESIGN

JOANNA TRADING

CHRISTOPHER NEVILE PARTNERSHIP

SIMON PLAYLE LTD

ROSSIE DESIGNS LTD

IAN G SHAW LTD

THE CHELSEA GARDENER

PARISH-HADLEY ASSOCIATES INC.

MANUEL CANOVAS

INCHBALD SCHOOL OF DESIGN

HOUSE & GARDEN

OSBORNE & LITTLE

ISID

DAVID LINLEY FURNITURE LTD

The British Interior
Design Exhibition:
Preview 1989

PAUL ATTERBURY

Manuel Canovas: Le Dernier Empereur. Visual by Sybil Anderson.

An exhibition is, by its nature, a compilation of contemporary ideas and attitudes, a fixed point in time that reflects precisely the way we see ourselves, the manner in which we interpret our past and, sometimes, how we anticipate our future. It is essentially a piece of theatre, a sensual experience to be later recalled, or perhaps quickly forgotten. The main excitement of any exhibition is exactly this ephemeral quality whose transient nature stimulates the visual perception. When an exhibition has come and gone, it leaves little but the memory, and the few tangible records of its passing – catalogues or posters, photographs and reviews, perhaps a mass of documentation – can serve only as *aides memoires*. Nothing can recreate, except in the mind, the visual impact of the original. Anyone with an interest in art and design of the nine-

teenth century must have wondered what the Great Exhibition of 1851 was really like. There is a plentiful supply of contemporary drawings, prints, photographs and written reports – indeed few exhibitions before or since can have been so well documented – yet all this material cannot bring the exhibition back to life. Nothing can replace the actual experience of being there. Similarly, only those who went to the South Bank in 1951 will ever know what the Festival of Britain was really like.

At this stage it is easy to recall the British Interior Design Exhibition, held in Chelsea Town Hall in May 1988. The enduring memory is the extraordinary dominance of period style and revivalism. The majority of the exhibitors had prepared room sets that consciously and deliberately played with the past and so the

David Hicks International: 'The Bedsit'.
Visual by Geoff Barnard.

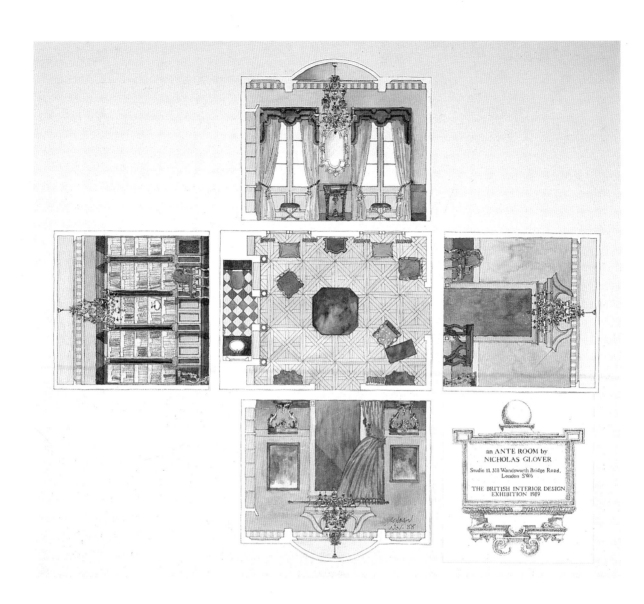

an ANTE ROOM by
NICHOLAS GLOVER

Studio 11, 318 Wandsworth Bridge Road,
London SW6

THE BRITISH INTERIOR DESIGN
EXHIBITION 1989

ABOVE *Nicholas Glover Associates:
Ante-Room. Visual by Nicholas Glover.*

LEFT *Broosk Interior Design: Dining
Room. Visual by Reg Trundle and Tony
Coolley.*

RIGHT *Mary Fox Linton: Dining Room
and Kitchen. Visual by Rico Nanty.*

whole display could be seen as a search for reassurance and confidence in the soft bosom of nostalgia. This was the year the country house look swept the board and the result was, in some ways, as deadening as the 1988 Presidential Election. The opposition parties, in the form of other style ideas, kept a low profile. Modernism, its increasingly unfashionable standing made worse by the cloud of Royal Displeasure, barely showed its face and there was little support for that most fundamental of design principles, the mixing of the best of the old with the best of the new. The new, regretfully, was rarely to be seen, and much of the old was mediocre.

The past is the natural playground for the interior designer, but the playing must be creative. To rely on mere

MC²: Reception Room. Visual by Caroline Aitken.

copying and the repetition of familiar old games is not enough, for the results quickly become inhibited and sterile. Contemporary themes must always be added, and handled with verve and confidence, if the design game is to make any progress. The quality of Victorian design, so often missed by its current wave of enthusiasts, is its innate vulgarity, its excessive exuberance, its love of colour and form, above all, its willingness to bend the past into new and often outrageous styles. It was neither discreet nor polite but it was supremely self-confident in the way it used the past as a mine of ideas, with no hint of the all-embracing nostalgia that dominates Britain today. Victorian design was essentially baroque, in the true meaning of the word, and it was precisely this element that was lacking at Chelsea Town Hall. This exhibition should reflect the style 'isms' of the 1980s in all their diverse forms: the neo-Palladian, the grand palazzo, the English country house, the new ornamental, the post-modernist, the minimalist, the Fifties' and Sixties' revivals, the Middle East, the creative salvage, the Italian contemporary, the post-holocaust, the decorationist, the barbaric and, above all, the new baroque. But many of these, if represented at all, were all but swamped by the tidal wave of commercial nostalgia.

The British Interior Design Exhibition is now in its second year at its new venue, and shows every intention of continuing into the future as a statement about design in

Britain. This second year is, of course, critical, for it marks the change from a once-only ephemeral exhibition into something regular, an annual comment on 'the way we live now' and therefore to be judged by quite different criteria. An annual exhibition is a far more subtle event, inevitably hard to separate from the one last year, and dependent upon a degree of change and progression to stir the visual memory. Annual exhibitions have to be powerfully and individually marked if they are to survive in the mind. Who, after all, can recall with confidence the precise characteristics of any particular Ideal Home, Decorex or Royal Academy Summer Show?

It is presumptuous to write about an exhibition that has yet to take place for the risk is to confuse fantasy and imagination with reality. Put more simply, it is easy to get it wrong. All those taking part in the 1989 British Interior Design Exhibition were asked to prepare visualizations of their room sets in order that this Yearbook could include a preview of the exhibition. Many have willingly supplied these, and they are valuable documents, revealing insights into the nature of interior design in Britain today. Drawings for interior design schemes, whether rough sketches or precise working plans, have always been important and often say more than the completed scheme. The shadow of the photograph now lies heavily over interior design since photography has ceased to be a simple recording technique, and the design process is now perceived in photographic terms. The tide of magazines, interior design books and commercial design catalogues has created a unified style of design photography that has come to threaten the nature of design itself. Now it is the photograph that has to be imitated rather than the camera simply copying what the designer has created. This is why the black-and-white photographs of Edwardian or Thirties interiors are often more interesting than the modern equivalents. To look at a photograph of a Syrie Maugham interior is to know what was there, not what the photographer would like us to think was there.

RIGHT *Mercier – London: View from Room 1508, Untitled. Visual by Georges Andraos.*

BELOW *Student Award Scheme: Gavin Renwick and Jaqueline Smith at the Royal College of Art: Case Study.*

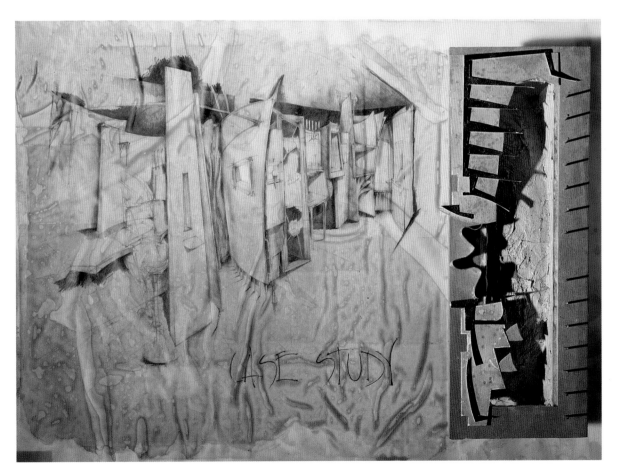

Guest Exhibitors: Bonetti and Garouste:
Hallway.

In the interior design field the camera can be seen to lie continuously, but the irony is that the lies have created a style which is now widely believed to represent modern design. It is universal, it is monotonous and it is ultimately deadening to the design process. It has come to a point now where many designers seem unable to think in graphic terms, producing visualizations that are drawn to resemble photographs. The language is identical, the same viewpoint into the room, the same cut-off foreground, the same carefully arranged piles of magazines and books, the same strategically placed flowers, the same orderly scattering of objects on tables. In a sense a revolution has taken place and the servants are now in control. One can only regret the passing of the old order.

ABOVE *George Spencer Designs: Atelier. Visual by George Spencer.*

BELOW *Scarisbrick and Bate: Drawing Room. Visual by Denis Fullerton.*

At the same time, the ability to draw is still an essential part of the design vocabulary, and it is one that is increasingly in favour. Many museums, notably the Victoria and Albert Museum in London, actively collect drawings by designers working today, and the selling of architectural drawings is certainly a growth area for both auction houses and dealers. The extensive use of drawings by Stephen Calloway in his book *Twentieth-Century Decoration* also helps to redress the balance. The drawings spread over these pages enable one to take a view about the 1989 exhibition, a view that is quite distinct from any judgment of the room sets as they

may ultimately appear when the exhibition opens its doors to the public.

The strength of the past as a primary source of ideas is immediately apparent and it is a little disappointing to see how universal the pursuit of the country house look has become. Nostalgia still outweighs the dynamic, or even creative, use of the past, and so the themes of 1988 are clearly still predominant. The strength and lasting quality of this style underlines a dichotomy in the design industry today. On the

one hand business is booming as never before and design is now an eminently marketable consumer commodity. On the other, originality is becoming rare, a reflection of the fundamental change in the industry. Traditionally the design business was entirely the province of a few highly educated and adventurous designers working exclusively for a limited number of enlightened and relatively wealthy clients, and thus able to control the public perception of design and taste at source. Now the role of the

designer is often that of the purveyor of instant, pre-digested taste, carefully contrived and packaged to suit the voracious demands of a public whose concept of style is a cocktail contrived by market forces, magazines and television. The results, inevitably, are efficiently produced, highly saleable and conventionally decorative, but they are sometimes as exciting as a Macdonald's hamburger, a product that is clean, neat, predictable, safely immunized against dangerous or difficult elements

BELOW *Designers Guild: Garden Room. Visual by Marianne Topham.*

LEFT *Parke Interiors: Drawing Room. Visual by Marianne Topham.*

BELOW *Beaudesert: Morning Room. Visual by Marianne Topham.*

PREVIEW 1989

31

ABOVE *Ian Shaw: Study. Visual by Caroline Aitken.*

LEFT *Alidad: Morning Room. Visual by Venetia Maynard.*

and internationally reliable. Indeed, internationalism is now a potent design force, but the need to create an internationally acceptable style can result in a rather tame product that has little room for genuine originality. It is vital to be able to incorporate into the design process elements from France, Italy, the Middle East, Japan and other different or exotic cultures, for these ensure the essential and continual development of organic change. Design has to be about change, the blending of old and new, taking two steps forward and one back, but at the moment there is a tendency to stand still and look firmly over the shoulder at a fixed point in time. We seem to be obsessed by the chintzy style of the late eighteenth century-early Victorian period, our view of the fashionable interior based entirely on those delicate and carefully coloured paintings of interiors produced in abundance by Victorian lady water-colourists in their long hours of leisure. As one of a number of historical sources they provide excellent material, but their cozy nostalgia now dominates many of today's designers. Indeed, it is uncanny how closely a number of the visualizations for the 1989 room sets have echoed these early nineteenth-century models. Hopefully, the actual rooms will reveal a more independent personality. There is, of course, nothing wrong with an appreciation of the past in all its forms and the best designers have always been able to make the most of their wide appreciation of art and design history. Creative design, whether it be neo-Palladianism, the baroque revival, minimalism or even the stylized modernism of Memphis, can only spring from a proper sense of historical perspective. The danger in the route taken by so many designers today is that, while commercially sound, it becomes by repetition creatively sterile, as revivalism degenerates into mere pastiche.

Any consideration of the drawings on these pages has to start with David Hicks International, whose design for a bed-sitting room incorporates and underlines all those elements that have made Hicks the master for so many years. Here is classicism used in the most inventive and original way, with a wealth of intellectual and historical allusions that make the drawing a complete statement on its own terms. It is a robust, entertaining and highly individual comment upon current stylistic dependence on a particular view of the past. Equally enjoyable, both as a drawing and as a contemporary interpretation of a view of classicism, is Nicholas Glover's design for an anteroom – French rural baroque in a pleasingly gentle style, but with plenty of academic references. Both Hicks and Glover share a concern for the decoration of floor surfaces, a theme that should emerge strongly in the 1989 exhibition. Neo-classicism is also the start-

Rosemary Hamilton: Hallway. Visual by Marianne Topham.

ing point for the dining room by Broosk Interior Design with its subtle colours and simplified forms, but the details have little to do with straight revivalism. The ceiling is unexpectedly baroque and the paintings also break the neo-classical mould, while the furniture hints at Sixties sources alongside the more predictable Regency elements. Neo-classicism and the baroque come together again in the design for a reception room by Martha Fellowes for MC², but here the classicism is in a stripped, post-modernist style, balanced by a strong element of intrigue and fantasy in the drawing itself. This underlines the principle that a design drawing has to have its own personality, independent from anything that may follow in three-dimensional terms.

Another interpretation of classicism is reflected by Mary Fox Linton's minimalist design for a dining room with kitchen, where mature high-tech elements sit well with stark neo-classical detail. These drawings suggest a degree of inventiveness and originality that was badly needed in the 1988 exhibition and indicate a welcome reaction to the domestic clutter and comfort of the early Victorian revivalists. Also interesting for the freshness of its approach is the linked living room and kitchen concept by Rory Ramsden at Blase Designs, featuring natural materials such as granite, wood veneers and silk in a style that has both post-modernist and Scandinavian overtones. Another unconventional concept is Mercier's design showing the view from Room 1508, an intriguing illusion with references to both classicism and Thirties exoticism, and potentially a worthy successor to their 1988 room which was a highlight of the previous exhibition. The point that interior design should be a creative rather than a repetitive process, in which imagination and fantasy are as important as historical reference, is underlined by the drawing submitted by Gavin Renwick and Jaqueline Smith of the Royal College of Art. This sponsored design, with its post-holocaust, creative salvage and Sixties constructivist references, shows that there may be a life beyond nostalgia. Refreshingly free from conventional classicism and other revivalist tendencies is the design by the French partnership Bonetti and Garouste, guest exhibitors at the 1989 show. Much of their work is an entertaining blend of colour and fantasy and their drawing, which echoes both the mannerists and naturalism in its own barbaric way, continues this personal tradition. This is another route to the future.

While contemporary design does at least make its presence felt at the 1989 exhibition in a far more positive way, the dominant themes of 1989 are still those of 1988. Many designers are still firmly stuck within the design conventions of the early nineteenth century, and some of the schemes are little more than an assemblage of carefully chosen objects in a suitable period setting with an inevitable emphasis upon textiles and the treatment of wall surfaces. It is the country house look suburbanized by layers of

comfortable nostalgia, but of course this is what successful commercial High Street interior design is all about. One has to ask whether some of these designers should be more honestly called antique dealers, for some designs appear to be little more than decorative sets for the display of choice furniture and objets d'art which are all, naturally, for sale. There has always been a blurring of the boundaries between these two professions but in the past the antiques have been there to complement the designs. Now it would seem to be the other

Meltons: Hallway. Visual by Hugh Robson.

way round, and the quality of design is bound to suffer. Nonetheless, some drawings are delightful in their own terms, as exercises in decorative historicism, particularly the atelier by George Spencer Designs, Robina Cayzer's Regency dressing room, the study by Morrow Reis Designs and Alidad's morning room with its colonial overtones. Also enjoyable is the garden room by Designers Guild, with its bright colours and flowery chintz hinting at Mediterranean sun. Again, there is an interesting emphasis on floor decoration.

One of the difficulties facing all the exhibitors is the complex layout of the floor plan. In a sense many designers have had to work within constraints that might not have been acceptable in a more conventional environment and so there is an element of theatricality in many of the drawings that reflects an illusionistic use of space. Some of those faced with awkward spaces such as hallways have had to use *trompe l'oeil* effects, the full impact of which is clearly not apparent in a drawing. Such effects, used for example by Rosemary Hamilton and Meltons, are indicative of another currently fashionable design theme with its roots firmly in the past, although the modern style is a rather delicate affair, lacking the bravura of the baroque and the whimsicality of Rex Whistler.

The 1989 British Interior Design Exhibition may well be remembered as the one that brought to a head the debate about the nature of interior design in Britain. Does an outpouring of chintzy, pseudo-late-eighteenth-century, Regency and early Victorian interiors represent a crisis of confidence, or is the willingness to drift along on the tide of nostalgia simply a sensible acknowledgment of market forces? Can creativity survive when the pale echoes of the country house style have been spread thinly over every suburban terrace in the land? Find the answers in the 1990 British Interior Design Exhibition.

Pimlico Print Rooms: Study/Print Room. Visual by Nicola Wingate-Saul.

Contributors to the British Interior Design Exhibition 1989:

ALIDAD LTD

BEAUDESERT

BLASE DESIGNS PLC

BROOSK INTERIOR DESIGN LTD

CARTER FULCHER TATE

CHRISTIE'S

CHRISTOPHER NEVILE DESIGN PARTNERSHIP

DAVID HICKS INTERNATIONAL

DESIGNERS GUILD

GEORGE SPENCER DESIGNS LTD

HARRY PALMER

HELEN COOPER

IAN G SHAW LTD

JAMESON DESIGN

MANUEL CANOVAS

MARY FOX LINTON LTD

MC^2

MELTONS LTD

MERCIER – LONDON

MORROW REIS DESIGNS

NICHOLAS GLOVER ASSOCIATES

PARKE INTERIORS LTD

PAWSON SILVESTRIN

VITRUVIUS LTD

PIMLICO PRINT ROOMS

ROBINA CAYZER LTD

RORY RAMSDEN LTD

ROSEMARY HAMILTON

SCARISBRICK & BATE LTD

SIMON PLAYLE LTD

ELISABETH GAROUSTE & MATTIA BONETTI

GAVIN RENWICK & JAQUELINE SMITH

BECKETT & GRAHAM LTD

RODERICK BOOTH JONES

Traditional Decoration Today: Revolution and Rut

JOHN CORNFORTH

*I*n the twelve years since John Fowler died, there has been a revolution in the world of interior decoration, but it has been much more to do with the expansion of the market than the development of a new style. Suddenly interior decoration has expanded beyond the handful of highly individual shops and studios in London catering for a small circle of private clients used to having things made to order. Shops are now appearing in towns all over Britain to foster the demands of a much larger public that is in the main anti-modern, anti-urban and nostalgic in mood, and used to the relative simplicity of ready-to-wear. At the same time there are new commercial pressures that restrict choice.

However, whereas in fashion haute-couture houses have expanded into ready-to-wear and licencing, with their success depending on the interrelationship of these three different kinds of business, in decoration only Colefax and Fowler is pursuing that route with three retail shops in London and agents all over the world selling their designs, many of which were introduced by John Fowler when he was running the business over twenty years ago.

That is not only an extraordinary story of commercial success, but of the dominating influence of one man who had matured as a decorator and developed a distinctive look. I hesitate to describe it as a style because his was essentially a response to, and an interpretation of, a very special set of circumstances. On the other hand it would be fair to say that his firm

The Dining Room at Badminton House, with new curtains of striped wool satin by Tom Parr.

consciously formalized it as a style in the last years of his life and has continued to deploy it ever since. Moreover, his own work, albeit mainly known through photographs, has been such a significant source of inspiration to all those interested in traditional decoration on both sides of the Atlantic that it is seen as being a style. His personal touch was, and is, inimitable, as anyone finds out when they have to repaint one of a suite of rooms that has been decorated under his personal direction, or when part of one of his schemes of decoration has to be renewed; and his approach has always been easy to misunderstand, in particular working up from the simple to the grand rather than from the grand to the simple. The rut into which almost all recent traditional decoration has fallen has occurred because of a failure to understand Fowler's grammar and the difference between his grammar and his vocabulary, which, as with any language, has to evolve if it is to remain alive.

John Fowler was an inspiring teacher and a powerful influence on almost all those with whom he came into contact, but being thirty years younger than him and knowing him only in the last decade of his life, I had the inadmissable feeling that his decoration no longer really suited people of a younger generation because even his simplest work was more elaborate than their lives. So when not long ago I saw an excellent recent essay in his manner, I was interested to find that it seemed to belong to the early 1960s rather than the early 1980s and already had a rather disconcerting kind of period flavour.

The special circumstances lay in the way a small circle of private clients, not all of whom had great resources, wanted their houses brought back to life after the Second World War, made comfortable and fresh and given a sense of timelessness in a very uncertain world. Many of his most successful commissions carried out between the mid 1950s and the late 1960s were never photographed because not only did he not seek publicity but he did not want to destroy the chic of exclusiveness or break the air of mystery which was growing up round him and which he enjoyed. On the

A London Drawing Room. Imogen Taylor, originally John Fowler's assistant and later his partner, 'pulls out all the stops' with elaborately fringed curtains of white Indian silk and undercurtains of striped cotton, a way of decorating that cannot be imitated cheaply.

other hand, many people (including the young David Hicks) learned something from gazing at the windows of his Brook Street shop, even if only the brave ventured to go in: it was like going without an introduction into a private house, where a rather distant young cousin of the family would be sitting in the hall.

From a commercial point of view the business was not a success as long as he ran it, but he had an unrivalled string of rewarding jobs involving fine houses, splendid contents and stimulating clients. But that kind of practice scarcely exists today, and the chance to help a great house, as Tom Parr has done so successfully at Badminton, is now very rare.

It was the experience of houses of that calibre that stimulated and stretched John Fowler, not only influencing his understanding of colour, texture and scale, but also producing many of the patterns that have become the basis of what is now thought of as the Fowler style. Not only are such opportunities increasingly unlikely, but his particular blend of preservation and doing the minimum, of restoration and decoration has tended to split into separate directions, with the most interesting aspects of the work tending to be done by people who are not decorators. This is not the place to consider the difficulties that arise from that separation, but David Mlinaric is probably unique in England in trying to keep the various directions under control, rather like someone driving a trio of horses that are all pulling against each other. At Spencer House in London, for instance, he faces an extraordinary challenge of restoration and reconstruction, decoration and furnishing. Traditional decoration has undoubtedly suffered from losing that synthesis and from designers having to refuse commissions that are rewarding but unprofitable.

Not only has the nature of interior decoration work changed, but so have the opportunities to buy old furniture, pictures and objects of all kinds. Light and pretty painted furniture in an aged condition and faded gilding, which is what John Fowler liked best, are now especially hard to come by, and almost every purchase is an expensive one, even for a rich client. Looking for things is no longer fun, but a serious and often depressing search.

Thus there has had to be a subtle change of balance in decoration with less reliance on objects and more on upholstery; and that has coincided with a narrowing of the range of fabrics at moderate prices. Once conditions eased at the end of the Second World War with the suspension of rationing, it became possible to find a profusion of grand velvets, brocades and damasks as well as plain woollens, and cotton and textured weaves, with chintz as a delightful foil with which to 'degrand' a room; and that choice still exists for those who can afford to use mostly imported materials.

But many of them are beyond the means of much of the new market, and decorators and manufacturers have taken the relatively easy way out by concentrating on chintz, producing a huge choice of often poorly printed patterns. Then too many are used together. John Fowler's use of chintz is often taken as the authority for that, but in his schemes it never formed more than one element in any of his subtly counterbalanced rooms, and he would surely regard the present craze as ungrammatical.

However, it is also relevant that there has been a general revival of interest in pattern and ornament. In the 1950s and 1960s John Fowler's enthusiasm for historic patterns and his use of them was novel, but fashion has now caught up with him through the reaction against modernism and the growing appreciation of nineteenth-century ornament and pattern from Willement onwards.

Similar problems occur in the use, or misuse, of festoon curtains, an eighteenth-century form that was revived by John Fowler for tall rooms with sash windows, astragals and dead light, as they could be pulled up almost clear of the windows. He would have regarded it as ungrammatical to use them with windows of plate glass or in attics.

When Fowler was starting out in the years after the Slump, he had to devise economical trimmings as an alternative to braids and fringes, which he could not afford to use on his jobs, but in his mature work his range of specially ordered trimmings was very wide and very detailed – and correspondingly expensive for his clients. Almost all of them are still available, but again they are beyond the means of the new market and in a different time scale. So most people have to choose between cheap imitations, which usually look pretentious, or variations of his economical devices that cease to work when they are over-used.

In all this photography has been both a blessing and a curse. The sudden improvement of colour photography and printing has encouraged a flood of magazines that have Aga-like appetites for articles, and there are simply not enough good decoration jobs that deserve to be photographed. There is a vast diet of photographs of unoriginal rooms in the so-called 'country house tradition' that make

play with a limited number of themes and ideas. So just as a restaurant that never changes its menu becomes boring, the eye soon tires of over-chintzed drawing rooms.

John Fowler always said that decoration was ephemeral, and, while he would applaud the contribution of Laura Ashley as earlier he had admired that of Terence Conran, he would be very depressed by what purports to be done under his influence and would, no doubt, only wish that decoration was even more ephemeral. He used to say in a strangled voice that he would pay *not* to have to do yet another flat in Eaton Square, and I am sure that 'chintz festoon curtains' would have become for him as much a term of opprobrium as 'brown furniture'. In a car he was very much a back-seat driver, but he would surely be right in thinking that too many drivers have missed the turning at the roundabout and are heading down a suburban cul-de-sac. He would be keeping a sharp look out for a new route and a new figure from a younger generation to provide a breath of fresh air for the future, possibly a modernist from Parsons Green.

Good trimmings, like this tie-back from Claremont, involve a high degree of artistry.

French Influence on British Design

CATHERINE HAIG

*I*n 1849, the Journal of Design and Manufacturers, previewing the French entries to the Great Exhibition, exhorted English manufacturers to 'perceive in what respects they are surpassed' and to 'remember and remedy the character of their own deficiencies ... that in 1851 we may not even be beaten upon the old French vantage ground – the realms of taste.' Historically, despite their traditional antagonism, France has always been a Mecca of style for the English and still, today, hardly a month goes by without some reference in the 'glossies' to interior design across the Channel. In return, of course, French magazines reflect the continuing fascination with '*le style anglais*' in France. This two-way traffic in design and ideas, not without an element of healthy rivalry, will no doubt continue but, today, as Europe theoretically moves towards unity, pinpointing the areas of influence becomes an interesting exercise.

Opinions as to the depth of French influence on current English interior design seem to divide fairly neatly along traditionalist/ modernist lines. To fabric designer Manuel Canovas, for example, the answer is categorically negative: 'in fact, it is the other way round. Look at David Hicks who has been an enormous influence in France for twenty-five years now, and then at Tom Parr and Colefax and Fowler....' In contrast, to architect Georges Andraos, who took over the famous French firm of Mercier and brought it to London in 1986, the English Country House style is all very well in an English country home but it is 'abhorrent' in a Paris apartment or a New York loft. He believes that the younger generation of professional English are moving towards the French idea of light and space: 'French rooms have always been more naked than the English, with glazed doors and large mirrors; the English are now getting that sense of light and transparency. With the advent of proper central heating, the English are at last starting to undress a little.'

Undeniably significant in terms of French influence is the physical presence of French design and designers on the London scene. The exhibition, Avant Première, staged at the Victoria and Albert Museum towards the end of 1988, allowed a fleeting glimpse of the very latest in French furniture – much of it never before exhibited. Two of the nine designers involved were Elizabeth Garouste and Mattia Bonetti, the highly successful duo who feature as the guest designers in the 1989 British Interior Design Exhibition. Bonetti and Garouste first came to public notice in 1981 when they showed their now widely imitated collection of 'Barbare' and 'Primitif' furniture. Six years later, they hit the headlines again when commissioned by couturier Christian Lacroix to design his Paris salon, and since then they have turned their multiple talents to a variety of projects, notably the design of an

A scheme for a Middle Eastern interior by the French interior designers, Mercier.

important exhibition at the Fondation Cartier, and the interior of the seventeenth-century château belonging to Bernard Picasso, grandson of the artist.

While French fabrics have been imported into England for centuries, a new development has seen several companies leaving the security of an English distributor to set up on their own: Manuel Canovas, formerly with Tissunique, now has his own showroom; Lelievre became independent from Textiles FCD in 1987; and early in 1988 Pierre Frey moved from Tissunique to set up in the London Interior Designers Centre. These join the ranks of French companies already well-established in London such as Nobilis-Fontan and Souleiado, not forgetting important English agencies for French fabrics such as Percheron, Claremont, Marvic and Pallu & Lake.

A number of French interior designers have also chosen to make London their base. Georges Andraos of Mercier puts this down to the following reasons. First, the advent of a socialist president drove a lot of money out of France and reduced private spending. Second, there has been an influx of affluent foreigners to London, many from sunny countries such as the Lebanon, Africa and South America, who, while they appreciate the English look from a distance, have a greater affinity with the French approach to light and colour and space. Thirdly, interior design has long been a highly respected profession in France ('if an

English boy says he wants to be an interior designer, it is still on a par with becoming a ballet dancer or a hairdresser') but, 'there is still room in London for interior designers who understand, and can work with, space and light, although of course there are hundreds of decorators who just adorn a given space.' Furniture designer André Dubreuil, who has lived and worked in London for the last twenty years, says simply that this is the last civilized big city in the world: 'Paris is beautiful but the Parisians are difficult to live with.' He studied at the Inchbald School of Design, along with interior designer Christophe Gollut, French Swiss by birth, Londoner by inclination. Partners in IPL Interiors, François Gilles and Dominique Lubar are self-confessed Anglophiles: 'We love England and the English and that is why we work here.'

Certain elements of French design are notably evident in English decoration today,

Vestibule of a house in Hyde Park Gate, London, by Jameson Design. This shows the French approach to decoration.

assimilated into otherwise essentially home-grown schemes. There is the seemingly endless influence of traditional French antique furniture (and, inevitably, its modern reproduction). Elegant, carved, and often gilded, Louis Quinze and Louis Seize armchairs appear as a counterpoint to loose-covered upholstery in numerous English drawing rooms and, similarly, many an English interior features a 'Louis-style' chimneypiece, either in marble or stone. Architectural designer Conrad Jameson, a confessed Francophile, reasons, 'Victorian architecture needs the French touch to lighten it – at Jameson Design, we consciously put French mirrors and fireplaces into Victorian settings. The English are now trying to renew relations which were allowed to relax under Prince Albert's teutonic influence.' French Empire is another style much in vogue though only played on the grand scale by a few decorators and dedicated collectors. On a more popular level, the French country look, complete with fruitwood *armoires* and pretty Souleiado Provençal cotton prints, has transformed numerous 'country' dining rooms and kitchens. Also, slowly but surely, the continental emphasis on hygiene and comfort in the bathroom has had an impact, few 'luxury' bathrooms being installed today without shower (that works), bidet and cool, clean marble tiles. Fine antique terracotta tiled floors and glazed ceramic tiles are imported in quantity from France and there, too, one can still find workshops casting Empire-style chandeliers, wall sconces and finials. The French attention to detail and quality remains legendary.

Historically, French fabrics have played an enduring role in English interior decoration. The Revocation of the Edict of Nantes in 1685 brought a flood of Huguenot refugees to England who set up the great silk-weaving centres in Canterbury and Spitalfields. Throughout the eighteenth and nineteenth centuries, English silk weavers went to Paris for their designs and, despite the crippling import duty levied on French silks in the eighteenth century, many still found their way into English homes. The Red Drawing Room at Hopetoun House still contains a French silk smuggled in to avoid duty and it is recorded that Clive of India travelled to Lyon to choose silk for one of his houses. Still today, according to Guy Evans, who has the agency for Prelle in this country, one can say that France and England are the two great centres for furnishing fabrics; the rest of the world follows. Manuel Canovas, the master of colour himself, believes that the French have brought a wider range of plain colours to the English repertoire, and Jane Bayldon, who runs his London showroom, confirms that, in the three years that it has been open, English decorators have become noticeably braver with colour: 'they are more used to seeing colour and to using it.'

Today's vogue for reproducing antique fabric designs draws heavily on France's extensive legacy of original documents. Sally Gritten, senior designer in home furnishings at Laura Ashley, points to several designs in the current collections that are based on French patterns, 'partly because the Ashleys lived in France for a time and partly because of the nature of the designs.' Two chintzes in the 1989 collection started life as 1860s French wallpapers, found by Sally Gritten at a sale in Paris and then adapted and recoloured by the Laura Ashley design team. Interestingly, the technique of printing toile de Jouy, one of the most enduring and much-copied French fabrics, now enjoying another revival in this country, in fact originated in Ireland.

Beneath this physical level, however, the French approach to interior decoration remains very different to the English and its influence, consequently, is much more elusive. The work of Stephane Boudin of the notable French firm, Jansen, for Lady Baillie at Leeds Castle in the middle years of this century is a case in point. An exponent of classical decoration in the grand manner, his style was highly disciplined and controlled, concerned with every detail right down to the colour of the flowers. These rooms are still extant, largely unchanged, a vivid illustration of French interior decoration of the period at work in an essentially English setting. Still today, Georges Andraos of Mercier believes that French design is characterized by more formal control of colour and greater use of light. He points to schemes carried out in the Seventies by Mercier in the Middle East; despite the lavishness and sheer extravagance of the rooms, there is order and continuity of colour and style. The French, he argues, will focus more on a particularly fine piece of furniture or a painting, making it the dominant feature of a room, whereas the English tend to be over-modest. More people employ a decorator in France: 'In England even the smartest clients do not want their houses "designed" so you have hundreds of decorators designing rooms not to look designed; in France, a scheme tends to state clearly that this *is* designed, for *this* particular client.' Many of the rooms in the 1988 British Interior Design Exhibition, he contests, looked 'as if somebody's mother had designed them – unresearched, low-key and unpretentious'. Christophe Gollut puts the

Lady Baillie's bedroom at Leeds Castle, Kent, designed by Stephane Boudin.

same point in more favourable terms: 'Here it is comfort, abroad it's looks. The English *"laisser aller"* attitude to decoration is totally abhorrent to the French who pay more attention to detail and finish – and who value perfection.'

Proponents of contemporary design in England, such as Mary Fox Linton, point to another important difference in approach between the two countries. Whereas here, contemporary design – and, in particular, architecture – has been under attack recently, in France the State plays an active role in encouraging new design. In 1979, the Ministry of Industry set up VIA (Valorisation de l'Innovation l'Ameublement), an organization

dedicated to promoting creative French furniture design and to enhancing the image of the French furniture industry both in France and throughout the world (VIA helped, for example, to present the Avant Première exhibition at the Victoria and Albert Museum). The State also commissions works on the grand scale: President Pompidou's term of office spawned the Beaubourg, the controversial new centre for the arts in Paris; early in his presidency, François Mitterand commissioned five designers to refurbish some of the private apartments in the Elysée Palace; public works such as the new Musée d'Orsay and the Opéra de la Bastille encourage the commissioning of contemporary architectural designs, furniture and decorative objects; and Mitterand's latest project is the (again) controversial Pyramid du Louvre, designed by I M Pei. Traditionalists argue that the modern Elysée furniture is totally inappropriate to the period and style of the Elysée Palace but, nevertheless, names such as Philippe Starck, Jean-Michel Wilmotte and Ronald Cecil Sportes are now internationally known. 'Money would never be put into contemporary design in the same way in this country,' asserts Mary Fox Linton, whose showroom in London displays works by several young French designers. 'It would far more likely be spent on restoration. Modern design should be used – after all, if our great-great-grandfathers hadn't commissioned modern design, we would have no antiques today.' Fundamentally, she believes that the French are just as conservative as the English but that it is all a question of education. 'If you do not know the rules of the game, it is very boring to watch, and it is exactly the same when it comes to art and design. Unless you are educated to understand it, you cannot involve yourself.'

Georges Andraos believes that there is a fundamental difference between theory and practice in England. He trained at the Architectural Association and asserts that education at this level in England is enormously exciting and experimental. 'When you leave, however, all this changes instantly. It is the other way round in France; the French have a great experimental history, summarized, for example, by Beaubourg which was, of course, built by an Englishman – who could only have built it outside England.' The French educational system for aspiring designers is, by contrast, long and arduous. Competition to get into the good colleges such as Camondo, Les Arts Decoratifs, Charpentier or Beethoven, is ferocious and a course in Architecture d'Intérieur takes five years, excluding one year's foundation study.

Attitudes differ as to the possible consequences of 1992 when Europe becomes one in terms of trade. Mary Fox Linton sees closer relationships developing between design companies in the same fields, although she points to the language barrier as a basic but funda-

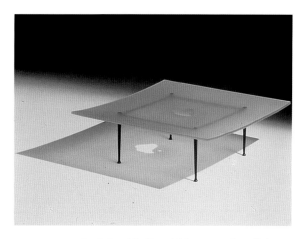

The Ikmisou sofa, designed by Pascal Mourgue and retailed through Mary Fox Linton Ltd.

mental problem. 'England with Europe becomes a strong force with a market-place the size of America – I hope we do not get left out.' Georges Andraos looks forward to the easy exchange of goods and labour but is concerned about the possible 'internationalization' of design. Others believe that little will change. Worth noting, of course, is the fact that 'Europe' means far more than just France: Italian design is still a major force, while Spain is up-and-coming with a mass of exciting young design talent.

Judgments on interior design inevitably tend to be subjective and perhaps nowhere more so than in classifying a national 'look'. Parisian-born Natalie Hambro, who now practises interior design in London, asserts that to the French, her work appears English, and vice versa. Christophe Gollut, whose work is described as English Country House with a Regency feel, gets the same reaction: 'I suppose I do bring something different to my English interiors, whether it is light or colour....' Wherever or however one draws the national line, there is undeniably an important network of cross-influences between the two countries which, with the imminent relaxation of trade barriers and the advent of the Channel Tunnel, seems certain to increase in the 1990s.

The Role of Craft in Interior Design

MARTINA MARGETTS

There has been much talk of a craft revival over the last twenty years but craftspeople themselves are often reluctant to agree. In this late industrial age, they are Cinderellas at the ball of mass production, allowed only incidental participation in the heady consumer boom. This is because their work is relatively exclusive, expensive and often highly individualistic. In this era, most interior designers have not rushed to buy or commission craftspeople's work.

It is important to distinguish between craftspeople who say they practise a trade and those who say they are artists. In general, the former will have undergone a traditional apprenticeship and will willingly work to an imposed design and specific brief, providing a service. The latter will hope for freedom in the interpretation of a brief and, preferably, early involvement in an interior design scheme, so that their creativity may assist in its characterization. The contribution of the artisan to interior design is covert, that of the artist craftsperson overt (if not extrovert).

Many interior designers have worked with craftspeople who can provide specific traditional skills – cabinetmaking, plastering, stencilling, hand-block printing textiles and wallpaper, gilding, forged metalwork and so on. But it is unusual to find interior designers who take a positive initiative to seek out, select and promote craftspeople with ideas, those who are interpreting traditional skills in a contemporary idiom, let alone those whose work is radical and experimental.

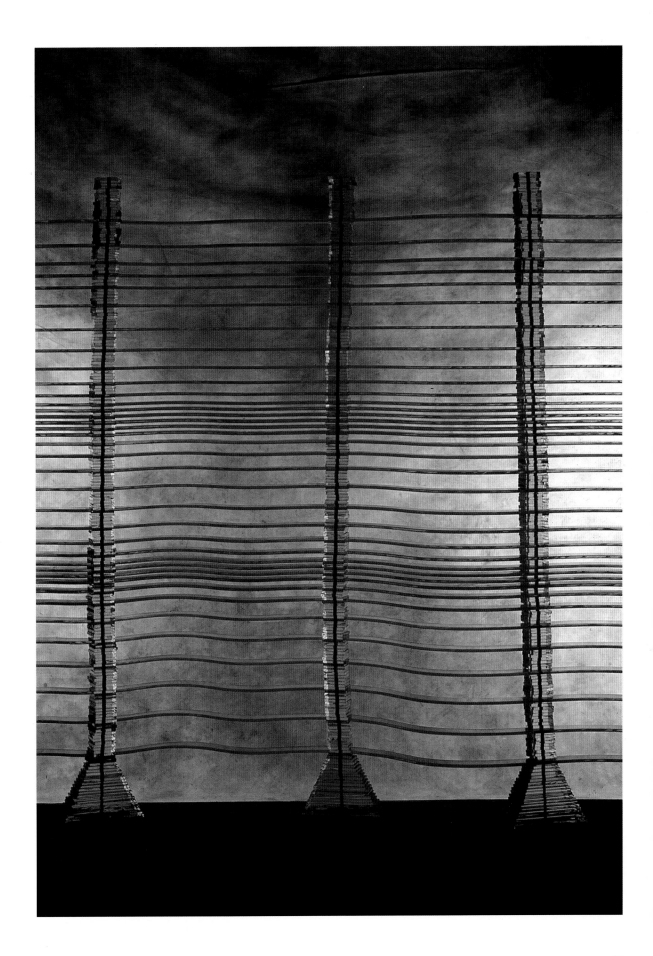

'Wandering Wave', screen of sandblasted glass by Danny Lane, 2.1m high, 1988.

It seems to be the retail outlets, some of them run by interior designers, who are most actively promoting contemporary craftwork, rather than design consultancies. Much of the interesting activity is concentrated in London. Mary Fox Linton and Tricia Guild, for example, reveal a discerning patronage over a wide range of craft disciplines. Sheridan Coakley, who once sold only reproduction Modernist furniture, has now made a success of choosing young designers of furniture and lighting, and acting as both manufacturer and supplier of their work. Jasper Morrison and Matthew Hilton, both distinctive late Modernists, have been his two main choices and their work has had a good response from Milan to Japan.

In contrast, places such as Crucial Gallery in Portobello and the House of Beauty and Culture in the East End champion the highly charged work in metals and found materials so memorably evolved by Ron Arad and Tom Dixon – the Post Holocaust/New Baroque/Mad Max aesthetic deftly exploited by the architect Nigel Coates for his bar and restaurant interiors in Tokyo.

This aesthetic seems to have struck as resonant a chord with the avant-gardists of interior design as Memphis did in the early 1980s. The backlash may come soon if the likes of David Davies, the designer who gave us the look for Next, have their way. His Covent Garden shop is moderate and well-behaved. Perhaps he is right that we feel more secure with comfortable furniture and teapots that pour, but dogma limits the potential of craft. (Visit the new Wilson and Gough shop at Brompton Cross for a breath of fresh air.) Craftspeople, too, have established shops to promote their work for interiors, such as Timney Fowler for textiles and ceramics, David Linley for furniture, The Glasshouse, and Wendy Cushing's new Soho shop for her outstanding furnishing trimmings.

In the 1980s, interest in interior design has percolated quickly to a broadening market, via Conran and Joseph and *The World of Interiors* to Laura Ashley, Next and the colour supplements. Although a demand for high-quality, more individual craftwork in interiors is gradually developing, at the moment even the visual professions need encouraging. Contemporary Applied Arts, an important exhibition venue and shop for the best British crafts in all media, now has a good slide index and commissioning service. It aims to attract interior designers and architects alongside other public and private patrons. It is under-used. Similarly, the slide index at the Crafts Council of England and Wales, a publicly funded organisation based in London, is also under-used. Yet it has the largest index in the world – over 18,000 slides – of work by contemporary British craftspeople.

This apathy might be an indication that most interior design schemes involve antique, reproduction, foreign or factory-produced goods. There is a widespread belief that projects involving craftspeople lead to expense and eccentricity. In the case of furniture by John Makepeace or Fred Baier – Chippendales of the 1980s – this will be true, but the likes of Alan Peters and Luke Hughes are in all respects moderate. (Alan Peters ruefully pointed out that his conference table and chairs for the British Insurance Brokers Association cost £3,000 *less* than the reproduction items the Board initially contemplated.)

There are many accounts of craftspeople beaten down by the British-patron equivalent of Arab horsetraders. The British may respect antiques, but often more as status symbols and as repositories of traditional values, than through any profound understanding of what is involved in fine craftsmanship and design. So contemporary craftspeople stand even less chance of discerning, consistent patronage.

Admittedly, crafts present a confusing image. The dichotomy between trade and art has bedevilled craft since William Morris. No-one is sure what the word represents or what is craft's intrinsic value or significance. Morris himself believed craftwork to be the noblest form of labour, exhorting everyone to pursue it in favour of factory production. Utopian that he was, Morris avoided acknowledging that the only handcrafts that were viable in a machine age were those which set the very highest standards of design and craftsmanship. By Morris's own example, crafts acquired a label of exclusivity when paradoxically what Morris wanted was beautiful craftwork for all:

1890s Kapps piano restyled and reconditioned by Fred Baier, lacquered by Page Lacquer Company, for Mr and Mrs Eddie Elson, New York, 1989.

Fruit bowls by Carol McNicoll, c. 23 cm high, hand-built of slipcast elements. Exhibited in her one-person show at the Crafts Council, London, 1985 (private collection).

Rug by Sally Hampson for Sedgwick Centre, London, 1.8m.

'Have nothing in your homes that you do not know to be useful and believe to be beautiful' was his maxim.

Initially, the Bauhaus successfully conjoined trade and art in craftwork by promoting handcrafted designs in textile, metal, ceramic and wood. But in the excitement of the burgeoning technological age, the crafts became merely prototypes in the laboratory of ideas rather than lasting objects in their own right and in the everyday environment. Sympathy for the hand-made, for the special qualities derived from an individual's handling of materials, techniques and form, ebbed away. The sleek simplicity of machined products and their potential universality caught the public imagination. Individuality was out, communality (the common good, the common aim, the common product) was in.

But the tables have been turning. The aesthetics of matt black and hi-tech, legacies of Modernism, continue to be influential

Wall clock by Gordon Burnett for the new N M B *Bank headquarters, Amsterdam. Oxidised brass, 37.5 cm wide, 1987.*

Light by Thomas Eisl, aluminium and woods, 2.1 m high, 1988.

Woven fabric samples by Joanna Short, various techniques, 1987.

'Over the City', etched/painted glass panel by Sasha Ward, 20 × 22 cm, 1988.

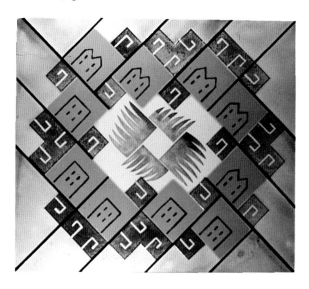

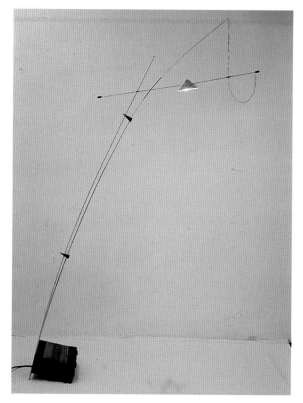

(interiors by Eva Jiричna, furniture by Rodney Kinsman, for example), but in Britain Modernism has never been the only creed. Contemporary British interiors are as likely to be variations on themes of Bloomsbury, Art Deco or Country Garden, an 'undesigned' vernacular popularized in the Fifties and Sixties. This eclecticism, or historicism perhaps, has

benefited craftspeople in the range of work available, but the climate has not always been auspicious.

The Festival of Britain in 1951 and individuals such as Elizabeth David, Terence Conran and, later, Laura Ashley, caught the post-war mood of optimism, of a freer, richer, more youthful and cosmopolitan society. The ethos was a mixture of the pragmatic, the romantic and the 'committed'. Peaceable, libertarian tendencies were linked to a search for naturalness in lifestyle. Contrivance and ostentation were inimical to the prevailing atmosphere of change and progress. In the free-for-all, fine craftsmanship was less applauded than do-it-yourself. Amateurish potteries and weaving workshops proliferated in the countryside. The status of craft was not high.

The 1980s, the Thatcher years, have seen a transformation of attitudes. Many more people seem to be willing to experiment with interiors, eschewing the 'heritage' style in favour of a flexible response to contemporary ideas. There is an element of fashion in interior design which seems more self-conscious and more ephemeral than hitherto.

In this climate, craftspeople can be cautiously optimistic. Craft skills which are constantly threatened with decline for lack of apprenticeship, and people keen to train, are enjoying a revival due to the interest in surface decoration in architecture and interior design. Specialist brickwork, marbling and metal patination are examples. Increasingly, craftwork is being commissioned for interiors of banks, hospitals and schools, and private houses.

Tapestry, stained, painted and sandblasted glass, lighting and forged metalwork are amongst large-scale commissions fostered by, for example, the Public Art Development Trust and Regional Arts Associations. And despite the sad demise of the Independent Designers' Federation, a group of seventy furniture and textile craftspeople whose specific aim it was to promote a relationship with interior designers, contemporary British furniture is at last being taken more seriously on the international scene. Types of furniture are also being revived in response to the fashions of interior design – daybeds, screens, candelabra. Many potters are responding to popular demand for tableware of bright colours and varied surfaces – sponged, sliptrailed, modelled and painted – while glassmakers are evolving graphic forms and exploiting the translucency of vivid colour in a range of works for interiors.

Given the essentially marginal place of craft in contemporary design and production, craftspeople can perhaps best, and uniquely, perform the role of a design avant-garde. The boom in the 1960s and early 1970s in art-school craft courses has produced a band of skilled professionals trained to think creatively and suggest a host of ideas in relation to the use of materials, techniques, form and function. Craftspeople such as Ron Arad, Tom Dixon, Carol McNicoll, Caroline Broadhead, Danny Lane, Thomas Eisl and Michael Rowe have moved the goalposts of craft.

Despite the inventiveness and professionalism of craftspeople today, many are undermined by the role of the architect in interior design. Historically, architects have often carried out the design of an interior and its contents alongside their design of the exterior (for example, Robert Adam, William Burges and Charles Rennie Mackintosh, let alone Gaudi, Aalto, Hoffmann and Frank Lloyd Wright in the international arena). Norman Foster, Eva Jiricna, Nigel Coates, Julyan Wickham and David Connor are merely our contemporary British equivalents. Individualistic craftspeople have fewer major opportunities as a result. It is fair to say, however, that architects such as Nigel Coates, Edward Cullinan, Jeremy Dixon and David Chipperfield are noted for their sympathetic attitude to the contribution that craftspeople can make to architecture, both inside and out. If the '1% for Art' lobby achieves its aim, the traditionally close relationship between architecture, art and craft may once again flourish.

In this coming period of boom and bust, of internationalism and freer trade, it is difficult to predict whether interior designers will hedge their bets with a homogenous international style or choose to emphasize national characteristics in craft and design with, in Britain, all the stylistic paradoxes of finely wrought versus overwrought, restrained versus outrageous, pretty versus ugly. Whatever their choice, interior designers would be well rewarded by a closer look at the range of contemporary craftwork on view at student degree shows, good craft shops, galleries and fairs, all of which demonstrate a positive, professional response to an increasingly serious and sophisticated interest in the craft world.

On Fooling the Zeitgeist

RODERICK GRADIDGE

*P*rince Charles remarked recently that in all the great periods of architecture and design designers have always been dependent on revivalism in one form or another. Quinlan Terry tells us that the ancient Egyptians based their architecture on Solomon's temple, the Cretans took Egypt as their model, the Greeks followed Crete, the Romans followed the Greeks, the medieval church builders were inspired by Rome, as was Vitruvius, from whom Palladio took his ideas. Jones followed Palladio, and Kent and Burlington copied Jones; Adam returned to relatively late original sources in Rome, whereas Pugin was inspired by English Gothic and so on into the nineteenth century, when more and more sources became available to designers. Morris reverted to simpler, more homely models and in this he was followed by the great Arts and Crafts workers, and architects like Lutyens. However, Morris was as much a revivalist as Lord Burlington and, had he lived long enough he would have had as little time for Pevsner's attempt at hijacking his ideas into the Modern Movement as his follower C F A Voysey, who in the 1930s went out of his way to disassociate himself from Pevsner.

It was not until 1912, when all modern art was invented, that the ludicrous idea took hold that there was something wrong with revivalism. It then became impossible to be creative in any style other than the 'modern style', one that had been invented in Germany to symbolize the early twentieth century. Over eighty years later we are still stuck with this style, and the thinking that goes with it. Like communism, the invented religion of the same period which has self-evidently failed but is still tenaciously held to as a belief throughout the Russian Empire, Modernism has now become a dogma. Although the results are nearly always inferior to earlier design, and are actively rejected by the people who have to use them, it is nonetheless believed that journalists and designers have a duty to continue to force this unpalatable style down the gullet of the lumpen public, whether they like it or not.

To suggest that a dependence on revivalism imposes a limitation upon innovation (always assuming that innovation in itself is a good thing) is very far from the case. All

designers work within some style or other, whether it be Post-Structuralism, or classicism, or the revival of the principles of the Bauhaus. No designer lives on an island alone, surrounded by a vacuum. The essence of good design is that it responds to its environment, which means that it must also respond to the requirements of the client, and through him to the requirements of the general public. Each project, be it a bright efficient clinic, a laser-riddled disco, or a library in a country house, must be met with a specific solution, and a designer who uses but one style lumbers himself with an unnecessarily cumbersome straightjacket.

Even if such a restrictive covenant was necessary for good design, the concept of a 'style of our time' is based on a fallacy, one that is no more than a foolish attempt to twist the *zeitgeist* to ends which it cannot serve. Any consideration of recent design history will show that it is impossible for a designer *not* to design in the style of his time. The style of 1990 may be quite invisible to us now, but will be immediately recognizable in later decades. One only has to look at carefully researched historical films made in the 1930s or the 1950s to recognize instantly, from details such as the cut of the clothes and the style of the hair, the decade, and in some cases the actual year, in which they were made. Similarly, the great Victorian Gothic revival architects knew considerably more than most people today about real Gothic architecture, often re-creating what they believed to be, and their contemporaries recognized as, exact replicas of real Gothic buildings. Yet today, not one of these buildings can fail to be seen for what they are – excellent examples of Victorian Gothic. Despite the aims of such architects to create exact copies of medieval buildings, they are in fact perfect examples of the style of their day and age. Likewise, the traditional inter-war works of Edwin Lutyens and Giles Gilbert Scott now seem to have more in common with the 'modern' designs of Oliver Hill than they do with, say, C R Cockerell and George Gilbert Scott, although in that polemical time no one, not even Lutyens or Scott, would have thought so. The *zeitgeist* will always win through.

Although it will not be possible to fool the

Addition in International-Modern style to The Firs, Redhill, by Connell, Ward & Lucas, 1935.

zeitgeist for long, at least we can attempt to create something that to our own generation will not be too offensive, and we can hope that in years to come our work will at least seem to belong to the building, and not look like an alien adjunct. The addition in International Modern style to a Regency house in Redhill, constructed by Connell, Ward and Lucas, still seems today as insensitive as it did fifty years ago when it was first built. On the other hand, Hawksmoor's designs for the towers to Westminster Abbey, built in what at the time must have seemed an alien and retrograde style, are now accepted as a natural Gothic part of the building. This would not have been the case had he used the Baroque style, a style that would have seemed more contemporary to him. To smash a modern design against an old building in the manner of Michael Manser or Connell, Ward and Lucas, is no more than an unimaginative cop-out by a designer frightened of history, made worse by the common justification that an architect has to use the 'modern style'. Unfortunately most designers today have been brought up to believe that 'history is bunk', and so have learnt only the minimum necessary to impress the culturally illiterate. Thus, they approach an old building in fear of the unknown, which more often than not can lead, by over-compensation, into destructiveness and insensitivity.

For most of my career as an architect much involved with interiors, I have had to face the problem of making additions to old buildings, from ordinary pubs (though no old pub is ordinary, be it a back street booser or an elaborate Victorian Gin Palace) to great houses like Hawksmoor's Easton Neston, Lutyens' Fulbrook or the North Wales castle of Bodelwyddan, which I have just completed for the National Portrait Gallery. In all cases the first consideration has had to be the original building, and how best to create a design that will integrate itself with the conceptions of the original designer. It must be emphasized right away that this imposes no limitations upon innovation, anymore than the original designer was limited in his design. But what it does demand is that one should, as it were, make an imaginative leap into the mind of a Hawksmoor or a Lutyens, and try to do what they would have done.

As a student of the Architectural Association in the 1950s, I was taught, though I did not believe it, that architectural history could have no influence on work today, and that the classical orders – and indeed all great houses – were things of the past and would be of no use to an architect practising in the late twentieth century. As it turned out, almost my first commission after I set up in practice on my own in the early 1960s, was the design of a new library at Easton Neston. I was introduced to the owner by David Hicks, who was redecorating the house. Hicks has always admired real classical architecture, and the design was done in close collaboration with him. Thus, for my first important job I had to teach myself how to handle the orders.

Hawksmoor's only house, Easton Neston is a magnificent miniature Blenheim Palace. In addition to the great hall, grand staircase and a large drawing room, there are three smaller living rooms. The main library is in a wing, said to be designed by Christopher Wren, away from the house. The Dowager Lady Hesketh, a great book collector, decided to turn one of the smaller sitting rooms into a library so that her favourite books would be easily accessible. The room is almost a cube (23 feet long, 19 feet wide and 19 feet tall; 7m long, 6m wide and 6m tall) with a pair of tall

windows facing the garden; doors face each other on the flank walls, one of which has a very fine late eighteenth-century chimney-piece. The room runs in *enfilade* with the central cross hall and the fine Rococo drawing room, so it was essential that the architecture of the new library held its own with the baroque grandeur of the rest of the house.

Since Hawksmoor had built no other houses, and thus no country-house libraries, the only reasonable source for inspiration seemed to be his magnificent Codrington Library at All Souls, Oxford, with its pilasters – Doric on the ground floor, Ionic to the

Roderick Gradidge's new library at Easton Neston, Hawksmoor's only country house, was inspired by the only suitable source, Hawksmoor's Codrington Library at All Souls College, Oxford.

The use of the classical orders in an existing room requires an understanding of their various rhythms, the 'Great Game' as Lutyens called it.

balcony – dividing the bookcases. The lower line of Doric columns became the basis for the Tuscan columns at Easton Neston, but to achieve the baroque power needed, the square columns are doubled one in front of the other, the column in front carrying its own Tuscan cornice and frieze with triglyphs, which return to the wall at the doors and the chimney breasts. The whole order rises to almost 15 feet in the 19-foot high room, a dimension arrived at by the horizontal rhythm of the columns and in particular the smaller module of the triglyphs. Using the classical orders correctly in an existing room can prove to be very tricky, particularly the Tuscan and Greek Doric orders with their immutably fixed rhythmn of triglyphs. This problem has taxed the ingenuity of architects involved with classicism from the earliest times, but there is no reason why the 'Great Game', as Lutyens put it, should not be played today, as long as all the rules are obeyed. There is certainly something very satisfying in working it out correctly.

To work on a Lutyens house can be even more satisfying since he took a delight in such puzzles, and built them into his houses. Fulbrook of 1897, in the heart of Lutyens country in Surrey, is particularly interesting since it is the first house where he used the classical orders. I was involved with a very considerable alteration and redecoration scheme here. When I arrived, work had already started on the designs of a 'modern' Austrian architect (my client was Austrian). This had involved punching holes in various walls to open out the plan. My task was to turn those openings into something that Lutyens might have created had he been given a similar brief. I also had to design a large covered swimming pool in the Lutyens manner.

Fulbrook is not one of Lutyens' best planned houses and the entrance hall was oddly shaped. This had not been improved by throwing another room into it. I tried to integrate the two rooms by creating a large semi-circular arch with a rusticated base. This was a favourite device, and in this case justified by the rusticated brick fireplace in the room, which I used as the basis of my design. I continued this form in an arcade of columns which disguised the cloakroom, using mirrors to enlarge what was a rather gloomy space.

The main problem at Fulbrook, however, was the drawing room. Here Lutyens used an Ionic order for the first time, and he used it with great mastery. Particularly witty is his combination of arches and columns at the staircase. A hole had been opened up between this room and the dining room, but this was sorted out comparatively easily by repeating Lutyens' order at the openings.

But it was on the other side of the room that the difficulty arose. Here an opening had been made into a small rhomboid-shaped room, with leaded windows to three sides, to create a bar. Unfortunately, the space thus created had visually little to do with Lutyens' main room. A bar did not in any case seem suitable in a Lutyens house and so I suggested to my client that this should be made into a drinks room, with niches for the glasses and cupboards for the drinks. I then discovered that if I took the arched detail that Lutyens had incorporated in the staircase opposite, and used this to form an octagonal room, I could achieve an architectural shape which would be inte-

grated into the drawing room. It was only after I had made this octagonal design that I saw Lutyens' sketch book for Fulbrook and found that he had originally intended an octagonal room here.

Bodelwyddan Castle in Clwyd, North Wales, presented a rather different problem, and one that was almost entirely a matter of interior decoration. Since 1920 this largely Victorian country house had been a girls' school. When the school went bankrupt some years ago it was bought by Clwyd County Council, and the National Portrait Gallery then decided that the main rooms would be suitable as an outstation for Victorian paintings. They therefore commissioned me to redecorate and refurnish the rooms in an appropriate style for their very fine collection of Victorian portraits. My task was hindered, or more probably helped, by the fact that all records of the house, including the names of the designers, had been lost in a fire in the 1920s.

On looking carefully at the rooms it became clear that they were by no means entirely Victorian and that they had been built at different times. There was, for example, some fine Georgian work and a lot of Regency Gothic. This became the key to the decorations, and also proved useful in hanging the portraits which came from all periods in the nineteenth century. In this way each room took on a style and a time of its own.

The entrance hall was patterned with stencils based on designs in Audsley's book *Polychromatic Decoration as applied to Buildings in the Mediaeval Styles*, and hung with false armour of the 1800s from Cholmondeley Castle. The next room was a long gallery. This was to house a fine collection of portraits by G F Watts, and so it seemed appropriate to decorate this in an Aesthetic, William Morris manner. Christopher Boulter painted admirable murals which suggest Morris tapestries. Beyond this comes the billiard room, which was to be hung with the original watercolours of Spy cartoons. It had thus to be extremely dark, and was lit entirely from light bouncing off the billiard table. There is a deep frieze here, in a Victorian/Elizabethan style, by Anthony Ballantine.

The large dining room is hung with late Victorian political portraits by major artists and here I used a splendid late Victorian brocade on the walls and for the very elaborate curtains. Throughout the house the curtains were based on original designs and in many cases the original working drawings. Their elaborate swags and trimmings add immensely to the feeling of authenticity in the rooms. The carpets also were rewoven to original designs in the archives of Woodward Grosvenor.

Beyond this is the library, grained to simulate dark oak, in a Victorian manner. Then comes the ladies' drawing room. The 1830s design of this room was inspired by the early Victorian portraits to be hung here. I used a fabric on the walls based on an original design of 1840 in the Warner archive and a tented effect for the curtains, taken from French designs of the period. This room is the only one

LEFT *and* BELOW *The Watts Gallery and Hall for the National Portrait Gallery's outstation at Bodelwyddan in North Wales.*

Visual by Anthony Ballantine of the Billiard Room at Bodelwyddan.

that contains any work by me, for here I designed the chimneypiece and the cornice in a coarsened Soane style to match the doors and architraves.

The next room is the staircase hall, which has a number of early eighteenth-century elements, including a dentilled cornice and a marble Palladian chimneypiece. So this room is decorated in a more traditional manner with dark green curtains and wallpaper from Watts & Co. Beyond this is the main gallery. If this splendid vaulted room, in the Gothick style of the 1800s, is in fact Victorian it is very retrograde. So the curtains here are based on those by Porden for the 1820s Eaton Hall, which is only a few miles away. The plastered vaulted ceiling has been painted to simulate stonework.

This was a very common Regency practice in such houses as Fonthill Abbey, but as no original examples survive today, it seemed worthwhile repeating this practice here, and the result has been much admired.

Whether all my careful attempts at authenticity will be appreciated by later generations is doubtful and in any case does not much matter, for however careful one is one cannot fight the *zeitgeist*. However hard I try, my work at Easton Neston, Fulbrook and Bodelwyddan will inevitably be seen in later decades to be as much a product of the late twentieth century as, say, the Hongkong and Shanghai Bank and the Lloyds Building. What is important is that my work should seem appropriate to my contemporaries today.

ON FOOLING THE ZEITGEIST

The Taste-Makers:
Design Patronage
in the late Eighties

COLIN AMERY

There would have been no Sistine Chapel ceiling, no St Peter's, nor would the young Raphael have achieved so much if it had not been for Pope Julius II. He was one of the Western world's great patrons and an inspirer of artists. Like so many of the popes he had always realized that much of the prestige of the papacy depended upon the splendour of Rome. From the Renaissance to the present, power and patronage have always gone together. Artists have depended upon the educated patron in order to thrive. It may be monarch or millionaire, leader or follower of fashion – the patron has an importance that is not always realized and often not recorded.

When it comes to the world of interior design – or what in less jargon-ridden days would simply have been known as the exercise of taste in decoration – the patron's role is fundamental. In the words of the old song, 'you can't have one without the other.' The professions of designer and architect would not exist without the exercise of patronage.

We live in interesting times in England. We are struggling out of the period of corporate and committee taste and decision-making into the more risky and promising period of individual and private patronage. The State has always had a crucial role to play. In the past it has expressed its own power or the aspirations of the people in the form of monuments or great public buildings. When we look back or visit the palaces of the past we imagine that they express some kind of shared values. Indeed the great Christian monuments still have power to inspire us but the private, domestic realm is something that in retrospect it is only possible to understand in part. Much more serious study is needed of the history of interior decoration. It repays diligent research because the interior world can sometimes be an expression of the mind of a period.

If I were an historian some fifty years hence looking back at the 1980s in England and the West, it would be fascinating to speculate about who would appear to have been the patrons, the influences that matter, the men of vision. One thing is certain: there are no great public monuments to admire in the Britain of the Eighties. You would have to go to France

where the tradition of State patronage of the arts has continued with strength. Paris would be outstanding – not perhaps for artistic innovation but for the number of large-scale national architectural commissions. A new opera house, several great new museums – some of them adapting historic buildings with verve and imagination; additions to famous monuments and new representations of a scientific world. All of these monuments have interiors on the public scale. It is interesting that these are usually untouched by the hand of the decorator and instead represent the international architectural world. The interior of the pyramid at the Louvre (designed by the Chinese-American architect I M Pei) and the inside of the Centre du Monde Arabe (architect Jean Nouvel) are both brilliant expressions of architectural technology and structural skill with steel and glass. The most intriguing great public interior of the 1980s is probably the conversion of the Paris railway station, the

The Pyramid at the Louvre, Paris, designed by the Chinese-American architect, I M Pei.

Orsay, into the Musée d'Orsay by the Italian architect Gae Aulenti. It shows off perfectly the preoccupations of the late twentieth century, our concern to preserve monumental nineteenth-century engineering and architectural achievements and our wish to use their great spaces to house the past in settings of the present. The work on the interior of the Musée d'Orsay, also by Gae Aulenti, is an exercise in Post-Modern taste on a grand, almost Pharonic scale. She flatters her patron – the State – by creating a great and monumental interior. In the same way, she flattered her private patron, the Fiat company, when she converted the Palazzo Grassi in Venice into a museum and exhibition space. Maybe it is because she is an Italian, but Gae Aulenti is an architect with a true understanding of the interior, both spatially and in terms of furniture and colour.

If we look at the great interiors of the 1980s it may be possible to discern both a stylistic climate and a climate of patronage. One of the major late-twentieth-century interiors is the Hong Kong and Shanghai Bank designed by Norman Foster in Hong Kong. This is on the scale of a cathedral of structural technology. The architecture is the dominant element; it dictates the design of the immaculate interior. In London the interior of the headquarters of Lloyds of London by the architect Richard Rogers has much of the same technical bravura about it, but it is less immaculate and less satisfying. These are two of the great examples of brave corporate patronage. The banks and brokers of the late twentieth century have the power of the Medici. But they differ in a marked degree in that they do not commission many artists to adorn their buildings.

THE TASTE-MAKERS

The museum is the public cathedral of the late twentieth century and James Stirling, the British architect, has thrived from the patronage of the museum builders. These patrons today tend to be a mixture of State and private patronage. The new wings for the Tate Gallery in London and the Staatsgalerie in Stuttgart as well as the Sackler Wing added to the Fogg Museum at Harvard all redefine the public interior. At the Tate the extraordinary colour schemes of the entrance hall and the con-

The new Clore wing at the Tate Gallery, London.

trastingly bland galleries are both strong statements of a powerful Post-Modern taste that has been very influential.

The National Gallery in London will be the latest of the world's great museums to have a new wing. This has come about through a direct private gift from the Sainsbury family and will be designed by the leading American architect Robert Venturi. The National

Gallery is also fortunate enough to be in the position to utilize the skills of one of the country's leading interior designers, David Mlinaric, who has been employed to oversee the redecoration and restoration of the galleries that had become seedy and neglected. The work at the Gallery represents another form of design revival which is the authentic restoration of historic buildings – utilizing academic and practical research in the service of accuracy and good design.

In Britain the National Trust has been a leading patron of the restoration of its own country houses. This has encouraged both debate and praise for the authenticity and effectiveness of the restoration of historic interiors. It is a controversial territory. For some time the Trust used the services of interior designers, concentrating upon John Fowler. He encouraged research, particularly into textiles, wallpapers and paint colours. He also imposed a style and his own work in private houses benefitted from his work for the Trust. The 'Colefax and Fowler' style was the result of this marriage of patronage and research and is a distinct contribution to twentieth-century interior design.

In the difficult area of restoration and conservation, patronage is often bestowed by the State. In Britain's public buildings this has not often resulted in a happy marriage of taste and bureaucracy. There are honourable exceptions: the Palace of Westminster is gradually being perfectly restored. In Britain the budget for buildings and interiors seldom reaches the

The Saloon at Clandon Park, Surrey, redecorated for the National Trust by John Fowler.

The Dressing Room at Beningbrough Hall. Both John Fowler and David Mlinaric worked on the redecoration of this National Trust house.

heights of expenditure in France. The restoration of the Palace of Versailles is almost an object lesson in lavishly funded accuracy. In Holland the total remaking of the house and garden at Het Loo is something of a landmark – re-creation almost taken too far. The privately funded restoration of London's Spencer House by Green Park, almost the last of the great town palaces, under the direction of David Mlinaric looks like being a fascinating example of patronage and carefully supervised restoration. It would be wrong to separate the patronage of history from the development of interior design – and in this Britain and France have a great deal to offer.

Patronage of decorators by the rich and influential in England and America has ensured the survival of the historically inspired interior, frequently based upon collections of art or furniture. Often the collection is made under the tutelage of the decorator or paid experts, who ensure authenticity and the application of the right level of taste.

Patronage of design by the commercial world represents a mixture of styles and influences. There is an encouraging new kind of property developer who has the refreshing maxim that 'good design sells'. This is as appli-cable to interiors as to office blocks. It is difficult for the public to see much beyond the atria of most commercial development but the boardroom floors of British companies often represent an encouraging mixture of strikingly modern design and more conservative taste. Stuart Lipton is the developer who has tried hardest to promote good design in the commercial world and his own offices have recently been designed by a very promising younger architect, Eric Parry.

Modern shopping leads to plenty of opportunities for patronage. As the larger super-markets cater principally for mass basic needs, there is plenty of scope for the small specialist shop to explore innovative and good design. The major supermarket chain of J. Sainsbury has built some distinguished modern stores – in London at Camden Town the latest example by Nicholas Grimshaw has won many plaudits, particularly for its vaulted interior. The young neo-Baroque designer Nigel Coates has not only designed interesting restaurants in Tokyo but also a fine, almost Gaudiesque jewellers' shop called Silver in London. Japanese clothes

The interior of Silver, the London jewellery shop designed by Nigel Coates.

THE TASTE-MAKERS

designers have offered opportunities for innovation with London shops by David Chipperfield and Stanton and Williams.

The world of exhibition design also offers scope for the exploration of ideas that are then adopted by designers for the interior, either commercial or domestic. Stanton and Williams designed *The Age of Chivalry* exhibition at the Royal Academy and created an interior that evoked the past while being entirely contemporary in materials and construction. Piers Gough is another architect who uses his talent in designing exhibitions, like the Lutyens exhibition, and creating bizarre and wonderful interiors for the world of money, made in development and on the artistic fringes.

In the more familiar world of domestic decoration, patronage remains much as it has always been, but with a recent increase of new money. The richest and perhaps most influential clients are still likely to employ the most discreet decorators. Little is seen of the work of Renzo Giardino, who is undoubtedly one of the leaders of what has been called *haut décor*. Like the late Geoffrey Bennison, he is not bothered by patronage but is in a position to choose his own clients.

The days of the single powerful patron who could commission something that would

change the artistic climate were on the wane ten years ago. Then Government and large corporations called the tune. Today there is in Britain a return to private wealth and with it a sense of adventurous patronage is reviving. It is too early to predict the outcome – tastes are catholic today and pluralism reigns. The richness of the feast is good for decorators. With the aid of that crucial patron 'the media', opportunities for good design and decoration have seldom been better. The climate for patronage is excellent.

ABOVE The Age of Chivalry, *the exhibition held at the Royal Academy, London, in 1988 was designed by Stanton and Williams.*

LEFT *The Boardroom, Lansdowne House, London, designed by Eric Parry for Stuart Lipton/Stanhope Properties plc, 1989.*

A House Resuscitated

JOHN STEFANIDIS

The controversy that rages regarding the environment has become a preoccupation of magnitude with the public that even politicians cannot now ignore. Genuinely innovative plans are sought, but new urban buildings when erected often lead to disappointment. The public objects to the brutal visual force that has dehumanized cities, particularly those buildings of the Sixties and Seventies, the result of ill-digested theories that date back to the Bauhaus. Good buildings by good architects elicit respect and create an agreeable space but there are too few architects of talent; too much fast building and commercial greed has presented architects with innumerable opportunities which have exceeded their gifts. The architectural profession is discredited as never before in the public eye. Nevertheless, some architects using high technology and innovative materials are successfully confronting the practical problems of the twentieth century which the classical fundamentalists, with a more limited range, cannot hope to solve. Saarinen's TWA terminal in New York has withstood the test of time, and the Charles de Gaulle Airport in Paris is breathtakingly ingenious and works. Classical motifs used for their own sake and not as an integral part of the building are not the answer to the demands of contemporary mass housing, factories or rail terminals. Amongst the post-modernists, whose trademark is often classicism, there are some notably talented architects, in particular Ricardo Bofill, whose gigantic housing schemes in Paris are a triumph of neo-classical concrete. This material when used by good architects, such as in Jack Diamond's YMCA Sports Centre in Toronto, can be beautiful and satisfying.

In cities contemporary developers surround their buildings with token gardens and too few trees. They plant their mean spaces without regard for human scale, and their buildings are often mere nods to the architectural movements of our time. But the developers are not entirely to blame for their poor aesthetics: such is the speed of communications that cultural movements which previously took decades, if not centuries to mature, are now public property within months the world over, and this leads to cross currents of ideas and styles which are misinterpreted. In architecture, it results in buildings unsuited to the traditions, mores or climates of the countries in which they are constructed. Le Corbusier's apartment block in Marseilles is a triumph, whereas in Chandrigah, his government buildings are a foreign blot on the Indian landscape – built in the opposite spirit to Lutyens' New Delhi, where he attempted an Indian style for the new capital of a sub-continent.

An Englishman's home is his castle. But the persistent failure of modern British architecture and the social changes of the last six decades has meant that a substantial, newly-built family house in a town, or in the countryside, is a rarity. In the last century, unlike France or Italy, the British preferred houses to flats (Norman Shaw's apartment block near the Albert Hall in London is an exception) and terraced houses since the eighteenth century have been traditional to English towns. The demise of domestic servants, or rather their hierarchy, has meant a new way of living in old houses. As a result of all this, the greater part of the work of an interior design practice such as mine is the conversion of old houses, adapting houses from another epoch to the amenities of contemporary life.

One of the most characteristic London house types is the stuccoed terrace, dating from the first half of the nineteenth century, and associated with builders such as Thomas

A House Resuscitated. The elevation of a four-storey house in Belgravia, transformed by John Stefanidis from a discarded Victorian building into a contemporary family home.

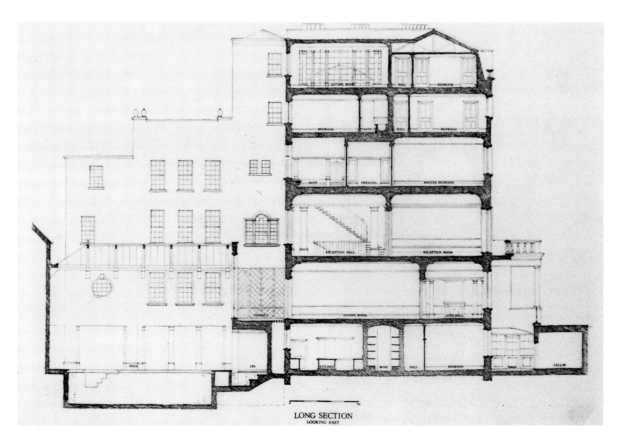

LONG SECTION
LOOKING EAST

A HOUSE RESUSCITATED

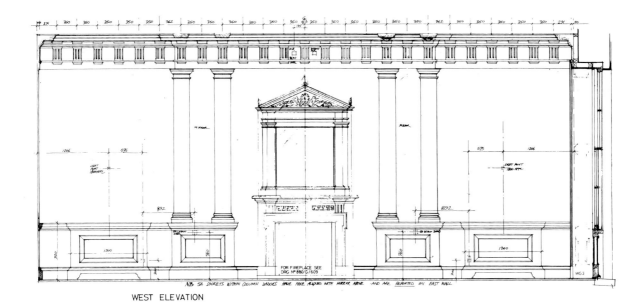

WEST ELEVATION

Cubitt. Victorian speculators gave London its present character. They were developers with a civic sense of duty, which made them build squares and communal gardens, and plant trees that made London an agreeable metropolis in which to live.

'Thomas Cubitt captured the imagination of his generation. He was the archetypal Victorian entrepreneur – the man who had started as a journeyman carpenter, and had made an immense fortune from an undertaking based on sound business principles. His million pounds was not made by grinding the faces of the poor, nor by shoddy workmanship in construction, but by enterprise, a high reputation for building, and a consideration for his workmen's interests, and for their sobriety and welfare, in accordance with the most progressive principles of the age. The greatest developer of his time – "the Emperor of the Building trade" he was called by one man who knew him – he provided much of the aristocratic London in which the later Victorians and the Edwardians lived their sumptuous lives. Belgrave and Eaton Squares are associated with him even in the minds of people who know little else of him. Most of the houses in Belgravia followed a pattern with a grand Purbeck stone staircase running from ground floor to first or second floors, lit by a glass lantern and frequently finishing before the top floor, which was reached by a lesser staircase, or by the back servants' staircase usual in most

On the ground floor, classical columns and a new chimneypiece restore dignity to the hall.

houses. Both staircases were usually of Purbeck stone, with, in some cases, the landings also made of long spans of York or Purbeck stone, with metal balusters. The accommodation was arranged in the way usual in all London houses of the period, with kitchen and service rooms in the basement, dining-room and possibly a study on the ground floor, drawing-room and other reception rooms on the first floor, and above this bedrooms with servants' rooms at the very top. Any variation would be provided, not so much in the planning of the house, as in the standard finish, the plasterwork, the design of the balusters, the fireplaces and the quality of the wood used on the floors.'
(Hermione Hobhouse, *Thomas Cubitt: Master Builder*, Macmillan, 1971.)

Our commission in Thomas Cubitt's Belgravia, typical of our stock-in-trade, was to turn a discarded and mutilated house into a contemporary home for a family whose standards are equal to their Victorian predecessors but whose needs are understandably contemporary. The house was a series of desolate rooms, divided and subdivided into dusty grey spaces filled with ugly utilitarian furniture, a cemetery of filing cabinets and unread papers. Fireplaces had been blocked, staircases had disappeared; there were notices scrawled on doors and small scruffy lavatories prevailed – an urban condemnation of the modern office at its worst.

A four-storey house with a basement, and high ceilings on the ground and first floors, meant a steep climb and necessitated a capacious lift. The height of the house demanded strategically planned kitchenettes: a family kitchen on the ground floor and a larger kitchen in the basement, which includes a laundry, staff bedrooms and bathrooms. Modern technology permitted a swimming pool to be built in a back yard, enclosed by a high roof of glass; changing rooms, sauna, jacuzzi and exercise rooms are adjoining and complete the basement plan.

Although the major concern was to bring back to life the house's vanished style, this was to be more than mere revivalism. In any case, there are Cubitt houses that still have their original interiors so it was not difficult to establish what the house would have looked like. It was more important for the house to satisfy the demands of a contemporary way of life, and so modern technology had to take its place. On the ground floor new columns and a new chimneypiece, carefully designed and carved, have restored the hall to its former dignity. A large dining room has been created to accommodate an extensive family, with a pantry and a family sitting-room with a small kitchen nearby. A lobby was built for the lift, and a cloakroom and cupboards surround the new stone staircase, embellished with a classical newly-wrought iron balustrade that rises proudly to the first floor ante-room. There is a library and also a drawing room which overlooks plane trees enclosed by railings, a typical city square of which London boasts so many. These rooms of generous proportions now have deep cornices, and panelled doors have replaced the remains of inferior 1920s alterations; chimney pieces with overmantels have been added, and rugs cover the centre of newly laid parquet floors. These noble spaces provide the suitable balance of formality and comfort the new owners required.

There are six bedrooms in all, each with

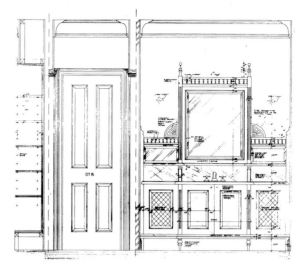

The top floor boasts a marble bathroom, an appropriate balance between formality and comfort that is echoed throughout the house.

ample cupboard space, of which four have a sitting or writing room, each self contained with an individual character to suit its occupant. A sitting room for younger family members has a glazed corridor flooded with light and looks over London roof-tops. The eliptic lantern at the top of the stairs had disappeared and was re-designed, larger in scale, and carefully re-instated in its original place. The top floor also boasts a marble bathroom and two guest bedrooms. The two floors below are of bedrooms linked by a new wooden staircase. The house's main artery is the lift, rather frivolously lined in sycamore. Cornices throughout have been invented or replaced. The natural progression of rooms with furniture in its rightful place makes the house feel as if it was originally designed in this way. I take this as a credit to our teamwork and the time devoted to the design of every small detail. It is difficult now to imagine that this large and comfortable house could have been offices for forty years. A poor, desecrated building has been transformed into what it now is only because British design and workmanship has improved immeasurably in the last decade, so that Britain can now boast as high a standard as ever it had in past centuries.

Design Profile

MANUEL CANOVAS

From an interview between Manuel Canovas and Paul Atterbury

PA: *Why did you choose to open your showroom in England?*

MC: England is the country where people are most interested in 'the house'. In France people are extraordinarily good at everything to do with the table, wine and food, but as far as decoration is concerned the English are paramount. So it was very important to me to be here under my own label, in my own name, as England undoubtedly leads the field in Europe. I think the reasons are complicated. Travel, and the influence of the colonies, have played an important part in English culture and history, and this has meant that people have developed a taste for houses and a profound understanding of decoration. For instance, in Europe after the war the first person of real influence was indisputably David Hicks. And I think that very often in the past England has been the country which has initiated movements. It is very avant-garde, despite what people think elsewhere. England is a pretty revolutionary country beneath its conservative appearance. In my sphere England definitely leads the field.

PA: *More than the United States?*
MC: We used to think that there was less culture than money in the States. Now there is a new balance. But it is true that people in the States are very interested in interior design, and in my view this is by virtue of the Anglo-Saxon in them; it is their Anglo-Saxon heritage. The more Latin the country, the less interest you find in decoration; in Italy the architecture is sublime, but decoration is non-existent.

PA: *In the past the exchange of ideas between France and England has been a one-way traffic, that is from France to England. Do you think that is about to change?*
MC: It is not about to. The influence of English ideas has been extremely strong in France for some time. And earlier I think it was not so much the influence of France but of Italy that was so strong in England. What with Palladio, the Baroque, the Renaissance and so on, Italy has left its mark on England, as it has on France. To the Baroque spirit the English have always added an element of exoticism – chinoiserie, for example. This is what has shaped English taste. The aspects of English style that have had most influence in France are those of comfort with elegance (not comfort in the classical sense, of course), colours, and sometimes exoticism. English influence is still very strong in France.

PA: *What do you think of English contemporary design?*
MC: I think that in contemporary design generally, and not only in England, there is a strong movement, now rather old-fashioned in my opinion, which is derived from the Bauhaus. Originally very beautiful, it has now become stark and pretentious, ugly and uncomfortable. This whole movement, which in some places is part of a Scandinavian and German, or shall we say Germanic, heritage, is now seeing the beginnings of a reversal. In France we see it in the work of the '*barbares*', a new Baroque, and thus completely opposed to

'*Marie Leczinska*', inspired by a French eighteenth-century fabric design.

Modernism. It is starting in England, which already has a Baroque tradition in its applied arts, and I am sure it will be welcomed. Somehow this cold, dry, hard Germanic movement will be submerged by the new romanticism and there will be a new Baroque renaissance.

PA: *Is it really a new Baroque, or is it just a fashion?*
MC: What is the difference between a fashion and a movement, a true, radical movement? It is a matter of how long it lasts. When I think of the Bauhaus I think of all those designers who made furniture, of Le Corbusier and Charles Eames for example, and their work seems entirely contemporary, although they made their furniture fifty years ago, sometimes more. Now that is really extraordinary, for they have now become classics. I do not know whether the fashion for the new Baroque will last, but if it does it will become a movement.

PA: *What about the frivolity of the Baroque?*
MC: The Baroque, as opposed to the severity of the Germanic movement, is a circle which has somehow become an ellipse, which already contains an element of frivolity. And then, like

all movements which have an emotional aspect, it gets burned up more quickly than hard, geometric rules which last longer. I feel that the Baroque, even if it does not last, is a humane movement, while I find that all the applied art produced by this Germanic movement has an aspect which is, how shall I put it, fascist, authoritarian, unpleasant. I do not like it.

PA: *Do you feel that interior design is by its nature ephemeral?*
MC: No, all art is important in all its forms, whether on a grand or a small scale. And it all links together to form a whole. If you think of the great Renaissance artists like Michelangelo or Benvenuto Cellini, they sometimes worked on a very modest scale; they would be commissioned to design the costumes for a fête while at the same time they were building cathedrals. Applied art is neither big nor small, but is part of a whole.

PA: *But surely interior design is now a more specialized activity?*
MC: That is very true. I am always struck by that when I think about painters. Contemporary painters do some very good work, but their knowledge is so limited. It is a reflection of our time. We have become ultra-specialized in everything, and so an interior designer is indeed only that – a designer of interiors. If our era has a problem it is the proliferation of things; we have too many of everything. There are also too many designers, too many people wanting to employ them, too many furnishings, too many pretty fabrics. We are being suffocated by too much of everything. It is the tragedy of the consumer society. I think that however many things are available only a few will be chosen. Those who are very good will survive, despite everything, and all the rest will be dismissed. Things are becoming hackneyed at terrifying speed.

PA: *Would it be better if architects designed interiors, as in the past?*
MC: I have known architects who designed furniture and everything else. It would be better, but then it was appropriate in an age when knowledge was more humanist. People were more open to everything. They were not specialists, so they conceived a house in its entirety. They took charge of the garden, they took charge of the decoration, they even designed the fabrics. And this continued until quite recently. Now, because of this crisis of super-abundance, people are obliged to specialize. Once outside their own little preserve, they do not understand anything about anything. And that is a big problem. It is a terrible shame to confine one's ideas within one specialized area, to lose the broader perspective. It is true when you walk round a town that the architecture frequently lacks unity. When I look at Rome, for instance, which I know well and where I used to live, there is an extraordinary mixture of styles, but there is also a coherence. It all fits together. But when you walk round Paris or London there are inconsistencies.

PA: *Perhaps the problem today is that designers do not have an understanding of history and history of art?*
MC: Yes, but it comes back to the same thing. In the past all artists, humble or great, had a high degree of scholarship. It was only when they had studied for a very long time that they then created. Thus they were highly know-

The influence of India in both colour and design is evident in vibrant checks like 'Burma' and 'Passy'.

'Delft', a cotton/linen mix printed with a profusion of tulips in vivid shades against a dark ground. (By courtesy of House & Garden *magazine.)*

ledgeable and cultivated. Now anybody can say after six months that they are a designer, a painter, a sculptor; they create three dreadful pieces, everybody talks about them, and there you are. It is a great weakness of our age.

PA: *Do do think that traditional art education is perhaps better?*
MC: Do you know what I like in the classical tradition of education? Apart from the ability to copy antique designs and so on, it taught designers humility, a quality which to me seems singularly lacking in the designers of today. They seem to be quite extraordinarily pretentious, and have forgotten that vital quality which true artists have always had. A classical education has at least this advantage, it teaches humility.

PA: *In England at the moment there is a craze for revivalism. Designers do not take the past and re-create it, they simply pastiche it. What do you feel about that?*
MC: I think that it is sterile. But the past to which you are referring is too distant. In England you had an extraordinary movement which referred back to the Renaissance, the Pre-Raphaelites. What they did had nothing

to do with the Renaissance itself. If you had shown paintings by Rossetti or Burne-Jones to a Renaissance painter he would not have understood them. But they transformed and re-created it. We have had too many wars, too many economic crises, and artists have lost their way, they have lost the thread. Today, if you take a composer, not a specialist in German music of the seventeenth century, for instance, but a good average composer, and you say, 'Write me a fake Mozart aria or a Bach parti-ta', he would not be able to do it. He will have lost touch with the spirit of that world. He can copy something, on the other hand, and he will interpret it well. But when you have cut the thread all you can do is copy. I believe the thread has been cut.

PA: *What can we do?*
MC: Well, I think the most extraordinary thing about our age on the positive side, and the most curious, is the way different styles of different periods and tastes exist alongside each other. People can be very avant-garde or very conservative in their tastes; they may prefer the Renaissance or the ultra-modern; every-thing is accepted, and exists simultaneously. It is what remains after a high tide; all of a sudden you are much closer to the past. There is also a very strong feeling in England, and in France too, for the past, especially for the eighteenth century, an extraordinarily classical taste. I think this sort of strengthening of our links with the past has parallels with the cycles of the planetary system. There are similarities between our age and that of the Pre-Raphae-lites, the neo-Gothic, in fact everything that was going on at the end of the nineteenth century. I hope that eventually it will produce something that perhaps we cannot yet see, but which will itself be a renaissance, a renaissance in taste.

PA: *What do you think about the contemporary idea of co-ordination in interiors?*
MC: I would say it was an easy short-cut to harmonization. Harmony is important in interior design, and everyone has a sense of harmony. Co-ordination is a short-cut to finding it. It is a solution. As far as I am con-cerned it is not the best one, but it is an easy

one. You know that *Punch* story about a man who goes into his bedroom, which has the same pattern all over the walls, the curtains, the sheets, the carpet, even his wife's dressing gown. He opens a drawer to get out his pyjamas, and of course they are in the same pattern again. Co-ordination is the opposite of originality, but it is the first step for people who do not have a very developed sense of style. They start with co-ordination, and later may develop their own style.

PA: *Perhaps this explains the success in England of mass market interior design?*
MC: Yes, because all sorts of things have now been co-ordinated. But it is also a way of neutralizing a décor, of sterilizing it.

PA: *It is a very safe style, creating confidence.*
MC: Yes, absolutely. For people who are just starting out, buying co-ordinated things is a way of being sure of not making mistakes. As in everything, there are those who will develop their own taste, and then there is the majority who wish simply to be reassured by those who are best at it, those who are most original and most courageous. In the decorating field, if I may make a criticism, I would say that generally speaking we lack courage. Beautiful houses, interesting houses, are always the work of people with originality and courage.

PA: *In England, perhaps because of the quality of the light, do you think we are afraid of colour, of frivolity, of mixing styles?*
MC: No, I don't because I think English people have a great sense of colour. I have seen English houses, grand houses or even historic castles, which have rooms painted entirely in yellow, or entirely in peach – that is something you would never see in France. The English are very fond of colour precisely *because* of the dull climate. They need colour. What strikes me in England is the amount of colour in interiors, and the judgment with which it is used. Look at someone like David Hicks; twenty-five years ago in France he would never have been able to impose the colour schemes that he has created here, even at Buckingham Palace. He could never have done that in France. I certainly think the English are more daring than the French.

PA: *So the English appreciate your fabrics, and they understand what you are trying to do with your designs?*
MC: The English are less *petit bourgeois* than Mediterranean people. Now many people do not like my fabrics because they are highly coloured, vivid, perhaps even a little shocking. But it is for precisely these reasons that the English like them. It is very strange. Take the German market, for example. It is much harder

Designs like 'Michelle' show the shimmering effect of stripes in contrasting colours.

Inspiration for colour schemes comes from a range of sources, such as skeins of fuschia slubbed yarn.

'Pali', a printed cotton with a baroque design of ripe fruit and coco pods that draws on eighteenth-century silks.

for my fabrics to succeed there because the mentality is much more parochial. The English are much more open. To southern Europeans the English seem very original. And I think it is true, the English have a taste for originality and for that reason they generally react well to my fabrics.

PA: *Have you used English sources for your fabrics?*
MC: Yes, indeed: chintzes amongst other things. Traditionally Italy was the leading country in textile design, especially silk-work, until the Renaissance. Then there was Lyon, followed by England and English prints. Why did England produce printed fabrics? Quite simply because of India; prints were a great Indian tradition. Yes, I have found much inspiration in England. Something I like very much in fabrics is a taste for naturalism, especially flowers, my favourite means of expression in fabrics. I was the first designer in France to revive chintzes on a large scale, both plain and printed. That was some years ago now, but I found the idea in England. The taste for nature was very pronounced and there are hundreds of designs based on it – especially flowers. Even if I re-create such designs in a different style, the inspiration is still somehow English. The taste for exoticism and chinoiserie, too, is extremely English. You would never find chinoiserie in a Latin country, but I love it. It is all part of the tradition of travel, in the West and East Indies, which has left such a strong mark on the country.

PA: *Your fabrics are very exciting because of their colours and the variety of their sources; their relationship with paintings, too, is interesting. I think this is something quite rare in England, perhaps because we do not really appreciate contemporary painting.*
MC: The only country that is really close to contemporary art is America. European countries are too conservative, and usually they mimic what happens in America. After the Second World War, the only country that managed straight away to produce graphic art was the United States: the West Coast School, Rothko and all the others. If I were trying to find links I would say that what these painters have in common with my work is unrestrained use of colour. They worked in a manner that was entirely sensual, like action painting, and it was very natural. This links up with an awareness of colours which you find in fabrics. In France this sort of painting is not very popular. A few bold spirits bought them twenty years ago, but now they are selling them to buy dark canvases by minor nineteenth-century masters.

PA: *Can people appreciate your fabrics without knowing the sources?*
MC: Of course, but their response is entirely instinctive, a reaction to the sensuality of the colours, or quite simply to the pleasure of them. It is true that a pink, a peach and a light blue together look pretty; it is a pleasant combination, like smelling a nice perfume or eating something that tastes good. It approaches the level of a purely sensory experience.

PA: *If you have any rules, what are they?*
MC: I have one rule only, and it is very self-centred. It is to do what I like. This is an absolute rule. I never make a fabric that I do not like, nor one that I would not have at home. I make fabrics purely for pleasure. I never make them saying 'Ah, people want this or that.' Never. I say, '*Tiens*, I feel like making an iris fabric, or this sort of fabric.' I really do make them for pleasure. That is my rule, and I do not have any others. I do what I like.

Formal Design
in the Garden

GEORGE CARTER

The enormous changes and innovations in art and architecture in the twentieth century seem scarcely to have affected garden design. To look at twentieth-century gardens is to find late nineteenth-century styles and attitudes continuing with only minor adjustments up until the present. What is it that has made this art form a stagnant backwater, cut off from the mainstream of art?

It has not always been the case. In the seventeenth and eighteenth centuries gardens can be seen as fashion leaders: they were the vehicle for wide ranging cultural experimentation and innovation. Gardens of the seventeenth century were at once museums, scientific laboratories and testing grounds for new architectural forms. In the eighteenth century the garden went further to become a political and philosophical statement, and the vehicle for new thinking about nature and the position of man vis-à-vis nature. Nor was the form of the garden itself the only expression; garden literature extended into poetry, philosophy and political theory, very far from the bland how-to-do-it kind we have now.

The garden has slipped from a prime position in the hierarchy of the arts to its present one which is, at best, a peripheral adjunct to architecture, and at worst a sub category of decoration under the uninformed guidance of horticulture. It seems strange that this should be so, particularly in a country famed as a nation of gardeners, where gardening is perhaps the most widespread form of aesthetic expression. As the activity in which we come to grips with our environment in the most direct way and which enables us to create our own ideals and visions most tangibly, garden-making has tremendous potential.

The influence of the Picturesque movement

The decline of the cultural status of gardens, and the crystallization of our present notion of what a garden is, happens in the nineteenth century, and is, I think, partly to do with a new and reverential attitude to nature and the rural landscape. The prime reason for this was the Picturesque movement, which started in the late eighteenth century as an aesthetic theory for an informed élite, but gradually took such a strong hold, especially in Britain, that its origins were forgotten and it became an unquestioning and automatic response to the whole of nature. What began as a categorization of visual effects in landscape, quickly turned into an associational aesthetic; that is, things that had been looked at within Picturesque theory only for their visual qualities became worth looking at in their own right as subjects, regardless of any visual qual-

Bird's-eye View of the House at Zeist *by D. Stoopendaal; eighteenth-century formalism in garden design.*

FORMAL DESIGN IN THE GARDEN

From Humphry Repton's Fragments, *1876. A new attitude to nature was heralded by the Picturesque movement.*

It seems to me that all the gardening movements that evolved in the nineteenth century, and there were indeed many, have been under the influence of the Picturesque view of nature. Such innovations as William Robinson's concept of 'Wild Gardening' and Gertrude Jekyll's 'Cottage Gardens', two of the most influential, are cases in point. William Robinson reverenced nature as 'never making a mistake', and Gertrude Jekyll enshrined happy rural England: that unselfconscious cottage life which was already disappearing by the late nineteenth century. There is of course much more pure art in Jekyll than in Robinson. She saw, for instance, the use of colour and form in planting in terms of painting, but this is heavily overlaid with nostalgia for a pre-industrial age. As a typical Arts and Crafts artist, this nostalgia was not just reflected in her gardens, but in her collecting, her recording of the past ('Old West Surrey' and 'Old English Household Life') and her craft activities.

Painterly use of colour and form in Gertrude Jekyll's cottage garden at Barrington Court.

ities. The landscape ceased to be looked at as raw material awaiting re-arrangement, as it had been earlier in the eighteenth century, and became something with inherent aesthetic qualities, redolent of certain social structures. The myth of happy rural England was born, and was celebrated in gardens as well as in art from George Morland to Helen Allingham and beyond. The highest aim of garden art became simply to imitate. It might be the imitation of nature, or the imitation of earlier styles, but it was certainly not within the remit of garden design to use nature's materials without reference to this fact.

It is this deep-rooted reverence for Picturesque landscape and the rustic idyll that has made it virtually impossible for us to see the point of seventeenth-century formal gardens. There are of course sculptural and architectural qualities in these gardens that we can appreciate now, but it is very difficult for us to understand the *essence* of them: they are so completely alien to today's idea of what is appropriate to gardens. They are often seen simply as an insult to nature.

Period revivalism from Repton to Barry to Jekyll to Lutyens was also rife, but like all revivalism looked at the surface rather than the underlying sense of what was revived. Even a thorough going architect/gardener like Reginald Blomfield was heavily influenced by the Picturesque, and saw the formal garden like Repton or Barry as an intermediate stage: a way of relating the house to the informal landscape in which it is set. Period revivalism, then, meant formality, but it is a formality very far removed from that of the seventeenth and eighteenth centuries. Effects such as quaintness or grandeur were certainly achieved, but these seem shallow when divorced from the symbolism, allegory and integrated style and form of their earlier models. Formal gardens became merely a style or a series of styles.

One can trace the longevity of the Picturesque influence in gardens by looking at the relationship between garden design and architecture in the twentieth century.

Gardens and early modernist architecture

The avowed aim of modernist architecture was to make a clean break from the past, but if one looks for a parallel movement in garden design, one is largely disappointed. The architects of early modernist buildings were unsure as to what sort of garden was appropriate and indeed on the whole paid very little attention to how their buildings related to the landscape.

This early period of modernism produced perhaps the most striking results, even if these were few. Some, like Robert Mallet-Stevens, proposed rather innovative formal gardens with geometric topiary, rather more radical variants of André Vera's Art Deco gardens. They grew out of his pre-First World War houses and gardens which were heavily influenced by Josef Hoffmann.

One of the very few early modernist houses to have a thoughtful garden was that of the Vicomte de Noailles at Hyères (1923). The house was designed by Mallet-Stevens and the garden by Gabriel Guévrékian. The garden consisted of a series of walled terraced enclosures with views to the surrounding landscape framed by window-like openings in the walls. Each enclosure was treated with a different sort

The Villa Noailles at Hyères, with formal gardens designed by Gabriel Guévrékian, 1923.

of geometric formality. Some were used as a setting for specially commissioned sculpture by Lipchitz, Laurens, Czaky and later Giacommetti. The house and garden were immortalized in the Man Ray film *Les Mystères du Château de Dé* (1928). This garden inspired one or two architects in Britain who paraphrased its most famous element, a chequerboard parterre, as at High and Over by Amyas Connell (1929–31) and Orchard House, Bristol, by A. E. Powell (*c.* 1935).

High and Over, overlooking the Mishbourne Valley. Both house and garden were designed by Amyas Connell.

The most common expedient was to place a country house in the middle of fields without any adjustment to the landscape, so that it appeared as if dropped from the air. Such a house is the Villa Savoye (1930) by Le Corbusier, whose aim here was to disturb the agricultural landscape as little as possible by building the house on *piloti* so that cattle could graze uninterupted below.

This lack of an appropriate sort of garden for early modernist buildings is illustrated by the well-known case of Behrens' house, New Ways, Northampton (1925), which was set in a vernacular revival garden (see Christopher Tunnard, *Gardens in the Modern Landscape*, 1937).

However by the Thirties it is informal Picturesque parkland that one generally thinks of as the ideal setting for modernist architecture, sometimes modified by an architectural treatment of the grounds immediately adjacent to the building. This exactly reflects the early nineteenth-century approach to the problem of relating buildings to their setting. In fact two of the most reproduced modernist houses in England, Joldwynds, Surrey, by Oliver Hill (1930) and St Anne's Hill, Surrey, by

Joldwynds, Surrey, designed by Oliver Hill and set in existing landscaped gardens.

Raymond McGrath (1937), were set in existing landscape gardens. The forms of the architecture were designed with the landscape in mind, following to the letter the principles of Picturesque planning propounded by Nash and his followers. The formal terracing in both schemes similarly reminds one of the writings of Repton and W S Gilpin, and indeed of later nineteenth-century writers on gardens who all insist on an intermediate formality between building and informal landscape.

Gardens and old or revivalist houses

It is surprising to find that before the Second World War the most inventive gardens were designed not for modernist buildings, but for old or revivalist ones. Two of the best practitioners were, I think, Oliver Hill and Clough Williams-Ellis.

Oliver Hill was of the last generation of architects that felt there was no anomaly in practising in a variety of styles. This had been a commonplace attitude in the eighteenth and nineteenth centuries, but is now felt to be not respectable by committed modernists. Hill worked in neo-Georgian and neo-vernacular styles as well as designing modernist buildings. The garden schemes that he designed for his revivalist houses adopt an equally eclectic approach, and forms from a variety of periods and countries are assembled in a delightfully inventive way.

A similar picking from this and that architectural style characterized Clough Williams-Ellis's approach to gardens. His most famous creation, Portmeirion, is a complete restatement of early nineteenth-century Picturesque theory, but most of his other gardens are grandly architectural and rely on axial symmetry. One of the best, Oare House in Wiltshire, relates to

Plas Brondau, Wales, home of Clough Williams-Ellis.

an early eighteenth-century house and contains a series of interlinked enclosures which reflect the period of the house. His own house, Plas Brondaw, contains a romantic use of topiary set against the Snowdonian landscape.

The most famous and successful gardens of the twentieth century have been associated with old buildings; Sissinghurst, Hidcote and Tintinhull spring immediately to mind. These gardens, though not adopting a new approach, have very successfully combined an element of formality with lush informal planting, thus reconciling the two poles of nineteenth-century taste represented by William Robinson's naturalism on the one hand and Reginald Blomfield's formality on the other. They are not revivalist in any literal sense but amalgamate various stylistic inputs from, for instance, an

ABOVE *and* BELOW *The White Gardens of Hidcote and Sissinghurst, both created by amateur gardeners, reconcile naturalism with formality.*

idealized nineteenth-century cottage garden and an Arts and Crafts version of seventeeenth-century formality.

These three gardens were all designed by amateurs and have a degree of commitment which one seldom finds in gardens designed by professionals.

Post-war gardens

The style of garden now thought to be appropriate to modernist buildings is that formulated in Scandinavia and America in the 1930s and '40s and subsequently taken up with enthusiasm by British garden designers in the post-war period. Contrast in texture, form and colour of plant material is all important. The informal massing of vegetation is given point by being set against formal but assymetrical hard landscaping. It is the same principal that made the Jekyll/Lutyens and Sackville-West/Nicolson partnership successful. This formula is of course a simplification, but it encapsulates what modern garden design is about. The plant material provides the interest, while the hard landscaping provides a structural framework. Within this there is scope for elegant composition and horticultural expertize, but little opportunity for more. What masquerades as an abstract composition is in fact a discreet compromise between art and nature.

The most influential post-war British designers were all formed in this mould. One thinks of Sylvia Crowe, Geoffrey Jellicoe, Lanning Roper and Russell Page. What I think these have in common is a desire to remain stylistically neutral – their ideal garden would be one that did not shriek at one that it had been designed at all, nor would it have very direct period references. It would certainly be difficult to decide, without knowing, who had designed it. Their approach is adapted to a variety of architectural styles, but what it suffers from is a blandness which arises from its very adaptability. This is partly the product of an undue reverence for nature and partly the result of the fairly recent establishment of professional status for landscape design. Its practitioners have all been keen like Repton, one of the first landscape designers in the modern sense, to establish landscape design as a distinct study with its own theories, rules and education system. Here I think is the whole problem of garden design now. It is taught as a narrow discipline with civil engineering and horticulture as its mainstays. The result is that gardens are workmanlike but uninspired. Today the best gardens are not designed by garden designers but by amateurs, architects, interior designers and artists, because they approach the problem with a mind unencumbered by the professional constraints of landscape practice.

Gardens and fine art

There have been a few instances of the influence of fine art in gardens in the post-war period. Roberto Burle Marx's Brazilian landscapes adapt abstract painting to large-scale drift planting using vibrant colours. The whole point about these gardens is that they have to relate to the surrounding landscape – they cannot function in an enclosed space. It is difficult to see this particular approach working in British scenery and with British plant material. One way such grand-scale effects might be achieved here, however, is through the organization of agriculture on an aesthetic as well as a functional basis. This surely is not beyond the bounds of possibility given the present efficiency of agriculture and its surplus production. The eighteenth-century *ferme ornée* sets a precedent for such an engagement, and the fairly recent concept of land art gives the idea credibility. A scheme under the title *Fields of Vision* attempts something of the sort, under the auspices of Eastern Arts and British Food and Farming Year (1989). This involves the commissioning of artists to produce large-scale constructions using bales of straw to be installed across the Norfolk landscape at harvest time.

On a more intimate scale, Ian Hamilton Finlay has attempted to put poetry back into gardens. His schemes even manage to comment on political and moral as well as art issues. There has been in fact a small move towards emblematic gardens in the last few years, Charles Jencks' own garden being a case in point.

This is one of the areas I have been interested in with Raf Fulcher and Elizabeth Tate. We have approached the garden from the point

The garden at Dunsyre, near Glasgow, designed by Ian Hamilton Finlay, whose work introduces poetry into garden design.

of view of sculpture. That is not to say sculpture in the narrow sense, but in a broader context. This has been an area of expansion over the last twenty years, with sculpture moving out of the art gallery to engage with architecture, the landscape, film and performance.

The garden designed by Carter Fulcher Tate for the 1987 Chelsea Flower Show owes its form to an idea – that the garden should be symbolic of the passage of day into night. A single idea can be a great assistance in designing a garden. It does not really matter how half-baked – it is simply something to hang ideas on and to stimulate the imagination. It gives one a focus for invention, and gives unity to everything from the basic form to the smallest detail of planting or decoration.

In this case the plan of the garden is related to the orientation of the site and the position of the sun. Thus one diagonal axis will be light for most of the day, while the other will be in shade. Following on from this, the shady axis was made to represent night, while the other symbolized day. The night axis terminated in a theatrical representation of the night sky, with moveable shutters which graduate into blackness. At the centre of this a sort of astro-labe covered in silvered lead discs alluded to the night sky. The planting of this area was blue and dark green. The daytime axis is open at both ends and is planted with white and light green. At the junction of the two axes a fountain in the form of a gilt copper ball made reference to the sun and the weather. Two carved wooden terms represented summer and winter.

On a formal level the spatial layout of the garden was designed to create as many vistas as possible, and because of the relatively small site, was divided up by high trellised hedges. None of these were at right angles so there was an ambiguity which made it impossible to perceive the ground plan at eye level.

One of the chief aims of this garden was to get away from the notion that gardens are for sunny, summer daytime. The garden should be seen in much broader terms and can be made to look well at night or in driving rain. The number of sunny days in Britain is, after all, limited and one should take this into account when thinking of the ambience the

The design by Carter Fulcher Tate for the 1987 Chelsea Flower Show, which symbolizes the passage of day into night.

garden is to conjure up. Melancholy – a mood much cultivated in seventeenth-century gardens – can be quite as agreeable as cheerful sunshine.

The garden at Gainsborough's House, Sudbury, in Suffolk, is in the romantic Vita Sackville-West idiom, but lacks focus or contrast, so a temporary scheme was created which attempted to alter its character. I provided two architectural assemblages which were intended to change the tenor of the garden. One composition closed the main axis of the garden seen from the house. The inspiration came from the theatre, and the idea to be conjured up was melancholic grandeur. A series of receding planes culminated in a shaded obelisk which contained a grotto.

Not only does this scenic device change the mood of the garden, it also changes the scale. The illusionism of the theatre is used to give greater depth to the scene. The sort of *repoussoirs* used in stage flats and in the foreground of paintings are here adapted to frame the view. It is amazing how a formal frame can transform even an informal view, giving it definition and apparent depth. This is one of the most important lessons painting can give to garden-making.

Similarly, the way that space is articulated in sculpture can be adapted to gardens to give them greater interest and surprise. Light and shade as well as volume can be manipulated. Thus a very simple range of plant material can be used to create very rich effects.

This installation was only temporary, and it points up one aspect of gardens not sufficiently exploited – their transience. With the seasons gardens change and grow, and advantage can be taken of this by making various elements portable so that one can change the composition to suit different seasons. This can apply to plant material as well as to hardware, and I therefore have a

Theatrical assemblages by George Carter at Gainsborough's House, Suffolk.

number of large containers for shrubs and flowers, and re-arrange these as well as the garden structures in order to achieve new compositions.

Garden exhibitions

A major problem for experimenting with new forms lies in the lack of a suitable venue for such an art in this country. The Chelsea Flower Show could be it, but it is hampered by its status as an horticultural society, and its emphasis on plants to the exclusion of everything else. Indeed there is pressure on garden exhibitors there to suppress all aspects of the garden not relating to plants. The event is also marred by a lack of aesthetic control and a vulgar commercialism which insists on presenting to the public what it already knows and thinks it likes. Another more recent venue has been the National Garden Festivals of which there have been three, but so far these have been too much in the hands of the landscape professionals. There is scope here for extending the fine art input into gardens.

For art to infiltrate into a mass interest like gardening must be good for both, revitalizing the latter and de-mystifying the former.

Hardy Amies on Fashion in Interiors

JANE MULVAGH

A heightened sense of historicism and health-consciousness are the two strongest themes apparent in today's homes. The past is a fashionable theme in interiors now that the rhetoric of Modernism has been debunked, its theories proved to be specious. Hardy Amies and I discussed this and here are some conclusions that we drew.

Q: *Do you regard historicism as a burden, an obsession, in contemporary interiors?*
A: No. Certainly not. It is the only possible way to design an interior because history is an expression of our way of life, and particularly the way of life of the English, which is intimately connected with the past. Historicism makes use of the lessons and comforts gathered from the past and also respects provenance. Provenance, a sense of continuity and belonging, are very important. Instinctively, a young couple will go down to the Portobello Road in search of old things for their home, to give it a sense of cosiness and age. In starting a life together, no doubt to have children, a strong sense of their roots is naturally expressed in their environment.

Q: *Are historicism and innovation, or modernism, mutually exclusive?*
A: They do not have to be. Any too faithful a period room is abhorrent, humourless. One has to show a discreet but determined mixture of the old and the new. I have noticed that when the young make a reference to historicism it is with wit, sending it up, such as hanging

an amusing piece of Victorian Gothic ironwork in an unexpected place. This is a creative rather than a strictly historical revival.

However, I do think that it is a sad thing that young furniture designers are obsessed with the past; they should be creating, exploring, not copying. Within the historically influenced home environment there is, and should always be, a place for modernism in sofas and upholstery, for it is difficult to find old soft furnishings that are also comfortable. Comfort, in an historical setting, that is style.

Historicism and innovation surely go hand in hand. Any historical revival is tinged with the style of today. When I first came to London in 1934 the modern style was Regency revival. I realized that one must understand period things in order to be able to adapt them to the age, so I had to learn about Regency. I studied not only the interior designs and clothes of the early nineteenth century but also its social and economic history. You have to understand the mores and reasonings behind the design of a period. Like John Fowler and Alexis ffrench, its greatest exponents, the Duke of Wellington, its high priest, and Eddy Knobloch, the leading collector, I had to become 'au fait' with Regency history. We were all preoccupied with Regency drapes and pelmets, Regency furniture and plain, masculine colours. We had

moved on from Syrie Maugham's all-white room which was really the debâcle of the Modernist Movement. Now texture and colour added depth to rooms set with pale, stripped (what we called 'pickled') or limed furniture. We had reacted against what John Fowler called 'brown furniture', that is oak, mahogany and walnut.

Concurrently, historicism was all the rage in fashion. But rather than adapting the Regency dress (that high waist just would not work), we all turned to the romanticism of Queen Victoria's reign; bustles, corsets and Victorian 'come hither' frou frou, such as fans and Dorothy bags. Gradually Victorian artifacts crept into the fashionable room as well, hand in hand with the fashion in dress. Also, as Regency furniture was very expensive, the inevitable alternative was Victoriana, which *Vogue* promoted both for dress and interiors.

Q: *What importance do you place on a classical education for the interior designer?*
A: In order to practise interior design I believe that one is certainly well-served by a classical education. History lessons are essential and one should certainly know about English history from the Stuarts onwards. Elizabethan furniture is too difficult to live with, too big, too uncomfortable and so interest and relevance in

Regency revival in Hardy Amies' London drawing room, designed by Alexis ffrench.

The workroom, Savile Row, c. 1951. Design trends in fashion and interiors run parallel.

Modern kitchen by Gwathmey & Siegel, New York, focuses on pared-down design and natural materials.

the interiors of the past starts with the Stuarts. By the mid-seventeenth century many Englishmen had spent time abroad and consequently Restoration furniture was very influenced by the French and the Dutch. Furthermore, William and Mary brought style and comfort to the English manor house, which is considered to be one of the most civilized environments to live in today.

A sense of the history of one's craft is also important. Interior designers and craftsmen should have a knowledge and understanding of the progress of their art. I think that it is lamentable that the classical arts education, with its still life drawing, technical lessons and constant awareness of what has gone before, has been replaced by the 'express yourself' style of teaching. How can you 'do your own thing' without a knowledge of what has been done before, the styles of the leading exponents of your craft and the technical possibilities that are available?

Q: *Is taste acquired or innate?*

A: I have come to the conclusion after years of consideration and observation that taste is seventy per cent education and experience. I will give you an anecdote which, I think, proves the point. I had just laid a bed of tulips in the country and invited John Fowler to admire them. 'They're hideous', Fowler retorted. 'Have you ever seen seventeenth-century, striped Clusiana tulips? They are beautiful.' As I had never come across them I could not compare them. You see it is a matter

of education and I was ignorant. Well, if you have never seen an old-fashioned rose you are going to think that a Whiskey Mack is heaven, aren't you!

Similarly, it is necessary to see many beautiful, elegant rooms, and not necessarily grand ones, to understand and acquire taste. You see, most people who are decorating rooms are imitating and reinterpreting something that they have already seen. Basically interior design is a lot of clichés, rejigged. It is all about people ordering things to create that picture in their mind. In this respect it is the *customer* rather than the designer who really has to be educated. Most architects that I have met are very unsure of their taste, perhaps because they are not as preoccupied with interiors as they would have had to be in the past. Originally the architect was responsible for the bone structure and the decoration, inside and out, of a building. Now the dressing, invariably of old buildings, is done by the interior designer.

Q: *Why do you think that Modernism has failed?*

A: Modernism failed for several reasons; it lacked provenance, it was soulless and has always been disquieting. Modernists were obsessed with artistic statements that were ergonomically unsound and stressful to live with. These homes did not simply integrate the modern for reasons of practicality and technical advantage; they also insisted on looking modern. That is a hard, ungiving environment.

All good decorating today has a sense of weight. That weight is given by historicism, and by heavy textures and colours. We are enjoying the taste offered by Bennison; those dark-coloured velvets and modern rooms that create a darker, more homely environment. It is a cocktail of Stuart style and the taste of Charlie de Beistegui and Arturo Lopez, who advocated the style of Louis XIV which is our equivalent of the Stuarts.

Like the fashions in dress, interior design styles are never a violent reaction, but a gradual process of evolution, from one style pastiche to another. Like fashion, there are moments of shock. Our taste for Regency before the Second World War had been a reaction to Modernism; romanticism was beckoned in.

Q: *What are the most interesting developments in interior design in this decade?*

A: Firstly, and this may sound trivial, I think it is the revolt against wall-to-wall carpeting. The wooden polished floor is now greatly admired. What does this tell us? The appreciation of wood demonstrates that we are preoccupied with things natural, hygiene and health foods. Oak, being a robust and natural-looking, unembellished wood, suits our taste for the natural, the healthy. Young men and women today prefer to look healthy than to look rich. Secondly, we are interested in the architectural quality of buildings, that is their bone structure, rather than the cosmetics of interior decoration such as overcluttered Victorian interiors. This trait is also evident in fashion; the healthy, pared down, unpainted look is admired.

The demise of formal entertaining is the other notable feature of this decade. There has been a consequent preoccupation with the kitchen and thus dining rooms are virtually defunct. We eat informally in kitchens rejecting the formal, multi-course dinner. This is a good thing, for it demonstrates our reaction against heavy, typically French, food and many courses. Also few still have the staff to entertain lavishly. The focus on the kitchen is also symptomatic of the young's interest in beautiful, well-designed gadgets. The modern kitchen has become a shrine to these artifacts.

Fashion and interior design have been affected by the acceleration of change from one style to another. Cycles pass faster and faster, historical revivals come and go with such speed that many run concurrently. At the most fashionable end of the market glossy magazines will advocate Biedermeier one season, only to denounce it the next. Surely this is symptomatic of two contemporary phenomena; firstly, vast wealth in the hands of those who are desperate to keep up with fashion, perhaps because they have no provenance, no sense of continuity of taste. Secondly, the emergence of the professional itinerant, such as the international banker, who will be posted from city to city and have to establish a home for a matter of months. These wealthy vagabonds rely upon the services of interior designers for they have not got the time to set up their homes themselves and they do not want to transport their belongings from place to place. They buy good taste and depend on others to supply a homely, if transitory, environment.

Interior design is also playing a vital role in the marketing of fashion, as the two become more closely associated with promoting an image of one's lifestyle. Minimalism was the message of Japanese clothing which was set in such pared down, almost empty environments that the message could not be misunderstood. The efficiency and visual effectiveness of the new Next retail environment in Oxford Street, with its range of colours, sizes and styles displayed on the mobile rails, is magnificent; only I would have put in some English oak furniture as a counter-balance, adding a pseudo-provenance and a Britishness amidst the modernity.

The sales environment has always been essential in selling high fashion; one only has to recall the attention and expertise put into the old couture salons in Paris and London. However, the Eighties have beckoned design-consciousness into the High Street store with a heightened sense of sophistication.

Interior of Next plc, Oxford Street, London, 1989, modernism in a retail environment.

The Process of Design

SALLY GRITTEN

*I*t is often hard to define the process of design. Inspiration and ideas can come from anywhere as the mind sorts through the great range of influences to which one is regularly exposed. Magazines, books, exhibitions, films, operas, shops all play their part, but the past is always the richest seam to mine, a bottomless pot-pourri of styles from which to borrow. One thing is certain, no one designs in a vacuum, and most designers fill the vacuum by looking backwards. At the same time, design is not an independent activity, for the end product must sell. A successful design will satisfy popular taste, but it must stretch it as well, security mixed with a streak of adventure.

As a textile designer with Laura Ashley, under the direction of Nick Ashley, I am dependent upon the past, and it is part of my work to track down suitable original sources. I may attend old textile sales in London, or old wallpaper sales in Paris, looking for eighteenth- or nineteenth-century fragments that can be adapted to suit current tastes. Sometimes the source can be less direct, something seen in a museum perhaps, or a photograph in a book. Even the great Victorian design manuals, Owen Jones' *Grammar of Ornament* for example, are still immensely useful, but in the end it is always the real thing that is the best source. A couple of years ago I bought in London a wonderful early Victorian patchwork quilt, assembled from a variety of fabrics from the 1820–40 period, and this has been the starting point for a number of recent designs. It is not a case of simple copying, for the original designs have to be extensively altered to capture the tastes of the moment. Colours are changed, patterns are simplified, elements from one source are combined with others, sometimes one small detail will provide a whole new design. It is a complex and demanding process of trial and error. And I have always to consider the characters of our various markets, for the colours that sell in Britain are often unsaleable in the United States, and vice versa. With any international business this factor is increasingly important, and in 1989 for the first time we are producing quite separate catalogues for the UK, USA and European markets.

The early Victorian period was particularly rich in design terms, and many of its diverse styles seem to suit the current mood. The quilt includes Regency elements, by then a bit archaic, fashionable chintzes, echoes of the Gothic and the rich colours of Victorian medievalism, some classical touches and some examples of the Rococo revival, then just getting underway. Designs inspired by the quilt include 'Louise' and more recently the 'Ludlow' chintz, the latter combining Renaissance cartouches with Rococo pastels. Another is 'Bryony', a simple single colour design adapted from the more complex, multicoloured and obviously French nineteenth-century original, while for 'Honeysuckle' a single flower has been borrowed from a design that included twelve flower types.

The quilt is clearly more than just a remarkable collection of textile samples for its style is in tune with contemporary tastes. Victorian ornament and colour, classicism and the softness of the Rococo are currently popular and many of our designs have been influenced by the textiles and wallpapers of the early nineteenth century, in particular those with a French feeling. The chintz revival has been strong for some time now, and it shows no sign of tiring. There is also a considerable enthusiasm for the Regency style, both in its classical and its more exotic forms and sometimes we have brought together the more formal elements of the Regency with eighteenth-century chinoiserie. Again, the sources can be very varied, ranging from a direct interpretation of a design in the Royal Pavilion, Brighton, to the loose borrowing of a pattern seen in a photograph of an eighteenth-century chair.

A new range is the Renaissance Collection. This is a case where the original idea came partly from an exhibition, *The Age of Chivalry* at the Royal Academy early in 1988. The strong colours, formal patterns and architectural detail of the Gothic style were the obvious design themes, but we wanted to do something a little different by concentrating on the Renaissance, which shared some of the same elements. The rich colours and flowing arabesques of Venetian decorative design were a good source, reflecting as they did fashionable classicism. At the same time we looked to more particular sources, notably the costumes

A nineteenth-century patchwork fabric found in Paris was the inspiration for a number of Laura Ashley designs. The glazed cotton print of leaves and berries shown above was translated into 'Bryony' below, a more contemporary design of simplified form and colour.

depicted in English Renaissance portraits. Again, an exhibition was important, *Old Masters from the Thyssen-Bornemisza Collection*, also at the Royal Academy, and in particular the Holbein portrait of Henry VIII. Henry's sumptuous costume embroidered in gold gave us the idea of a single colour stripe in a linear classical style printed in gold on turkey red, and the result was 'Arabesque'. We also looked at books of Renaissance ornament.

Paintings have inspired other designs in the collection. A portrait of Queen Elizabeth I by Nicholas Hilliard shows the Queen in a black velvet bodice covered overall with a formal lattice pattern of gold braid studded with pearls. Freely adapted and richly coloured, this turned into a decorative textile, 'Elizabeth', with a simplified but complementary wallpaper, all in early Victorian Puginesque tones. Another design was taken from the pattern on the breeches in Hilliard's portrait of Sir Robert Dudley, while even minor examples of Renaissance decorative design, such as the inlaid pattern on a North Italian sword hilt, could start the design process rolling. The 'Tudor Trellis' pattern, by

Holbein's portrait of Henry VIII provided inspiration for the design 'Arabesque', which draws on the motif in his tunic. Queen Elizabeth I loved to contrast white pearls against black, silver and gold. Her black velvet bodice in Hilliard's portrait of her was the source of the design 'Elizabeth', named after her.

contrast, came directly from a French design manual of about 1840 and in some ways these nineteenth-century versions of Renaissance and Gothic ornament are closer to current tastes, and more easily assimilated.

Another valuable source of ideas are country houses, simply because they are still so full of wonderful things from many periods. There is an astonishing wealth of eighteenth-century textiles and wallpapers still to be seen, virtually unchanged from the day they were installed, but nineteenth-century examples can be just as interesting. Chatsworth has been the inspiration for a number of our prints including 'Derby', from the Chatsworth Library, and 'Priory'. I was also very taken by the Clive of India display at Powis Castle. Museum collections, too, are immensely important and the Victoria and Albert Museum in London is very helpful in giving information on textiles. It is

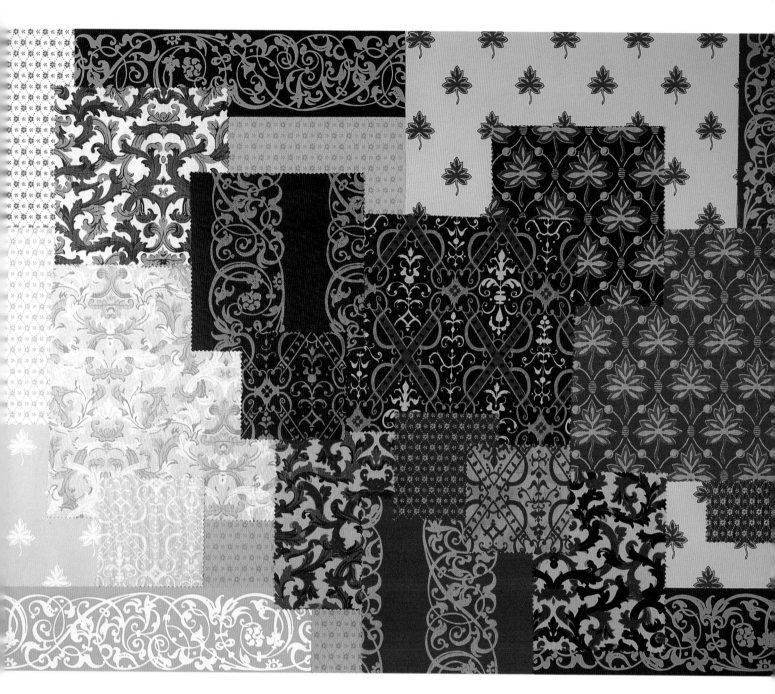

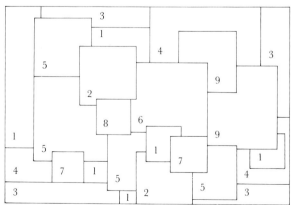

Laura Ashley's Renaissance Collection

1 Tudor Trellis
2 Arabesque
3 Arabesque Border
4 Darnley
5 Ludlow
6 Wolsey
7 Hilliard
8 Seymour
9 Elizabeth

The Clive of India Room at Powis Castle with its Gothic motifs.

often just the small details of an old design that provide the ideas. The colour is less important because we can always change that. Generally I am not looking for something that can be copied or revived, for this is not particularly commercial and in any case rarely matches popular taste, but there are exceptions. A recent visit to the Musée des Arts Decoratifs in Paris produced some eighteenth-century French wallpapers that we decided to use virtually unchanged for our Reveillon Collection. As this year is the bicentenary of the French Revolution, we thought it would be a good idea to produce a collection based on French eighteenth-century designs. We were very excited by the delicacy, femininity and wit of

the originals and could see that some of the simple floral elements used in conjunction with the grandeur of the originals would be just right for our style. One of the designs was even dated 1789 which was perfect.

Of course, the most important event of 1989 is the launch of our Home range, a complete lifestyle package that includes furniture, upholstery, ceramics, glassware, lighting and floor tiles. I have not been involved directly in the design of the range, but clearly co-ordination with textiles and wallpapers is vital. The

Gothic-style furniture, with its use of the pointed arch, is part of the new Laura Ashley Home range for 1989.

ideas have been drawn from similar sources, particularly the late eighteenth century and early Victorian period. The oak range, a blend of Tudor and Gothic styles unified by the idea of the pointed arch, springs from the same basic source as the Renaissance Collection, while the decorated walnut range combines Regency shapes with painted ornamentation in a late eighteenth-century style. The Edwardian range is a group of furniture painted in delicate tones that mix the light colours of the turn of the century with a hint of Arts and Crafts. There is a strong Scandinavian influence, with the distressed paint finishes echoing the interiors painted by Carl Larsson. A number of exhibitions with an Edwardian flavour provide the background, going back to Lutyens at the Hayward Gallery in 1984, but exhibitions have also focused attention on Scandinavia and particularly Sweden. Several more are due to open this year, notably at the Victoria and Albert Museum, and so Swedish design could provide several pointers to the future.

Design Calendar

*D*esign ideas come from many sources but exhibitions are always particularly valuable and 1988 provided a number whose impact in design terms may well be felt over the next year or so.

The Edwardian theme, already well established, was underlined by the rather quixotic *Edwardian Era* at the Barbican, and by Cheltenham Art Gallery's celebration of the centenary of C R Ashbee's *Guild Of Handicraft*. It was still possible to catch the *Arts and Crafts Movement in America* in Detroit, but the jolliest Edwardian show of the year was *The Painters of Camden Town*, at Christie's in London.

A new theme, Gothic and Renaissance design, was launched by *The Age of Chivalry* at the Royal Academy, and strongly supported by *Old Masters from the Thyssen-Bornemisza Collection* also at the Academy, and by the Armada exhibition at the National Maritime Museum. Renaissance-inspired decorative design will be important in 1989, expanding current enthusiasms for classicism in all its forms.

A number of more exotic exhibitions supplied a variety of design ideas, notably *Suleiman the Magnificent* at the British Museum. That Museum's show of Japanese prints, *Ukiyoe: Images of Unknown Japan* was also exciting. The impact of Japanese art in Europe in the nineteenth century was underlined in a colourful way by *Toulouse-Lautrec's Graphic Works*, at the Royal Academy. More unusual, but also potentially useful were *The Phoenicians*, in Venice, and an exhibition of Australian Aboriginal Art in Brighton. A highly decorative European view of the Middle East was supplied by Birmingham's exhibition devoted to the Victorian paintings of J F Lewis.

Some exhibitions particularly emphasized the current taste for the early Victorian period, notably the *Age of the Bourgeoisie* in Vienna, with all its Biedermeier furniture, and the display of Haussman fabrics in Strasbourg, while contemporary interest in botanical prints was given a boost by the Joseph Banks flower studies in the Natural History Museum's *The British Discovery of Australia*.

Hardest to assess in terms of their design impact are always the exhibitions of the twentieth century, exciting to look at, but often unpredictable in design terms. Notable in 1988 were *Late Picasso*, at the Pompidou Centre and the Tate, *Degas* in Paris and New York and the bright *Hockney* retrospective at the Tate. The Pompidou Centre's *Art of the 1950s* may indicate that a revival of the styles of this difficult decade is now entering the big time.

Looking ahead, the exhibitions due to open in 1989 are full of promise and they might indicate some design ideas worth watching over the next few years. The Renaissance theme could well be strengthened by exhibitions devoted to *Painting in Sienna*, at the Metropolitan Museum in New York, to *Leonardo* at the Hayward, and to the *Drawings of Michelangelo*, in Paris. *Royal Treasures of Sweden*, at the Royal Academy, may be full of useful decorative detail. The taste for classicism and the eighteenth century in general could be expanded by *Goya*, in New York, the vogue for all things Russian by *100 Years of Russian Art* at the Barbican in London. The great *Gauguin* retrospective comes to the Grand Palais, Paris, but the top style guide exhibitions of 1989 could be *Italian Art in the 20th Century* at the Royal Academy, *Miro* at the Whitechapel, *Latin-American Art* at the Hayward, and finally the important *Cubism* show that opens in New York in September.

ABOVE *From* 100 Years of Russian Art, *Barbican Art Gallery, London*

RIGHT *From* Latin American Art, *Hayward Gallery, London*

Exhibitions for 1989

DEGAS
Metropolitan Museum of Art, 82nd Street and Fifth Avenue, New York Until 8 January 1989

HOCKNEY
Tate Gallery, Millbank, London SW1 27 October 1988–8 January 1989

TOULOUSE-LAUTREC'S GRAPHIC WORKS
Royal Academy of Arts, Piccadilly, London W1 14 October 1988–5 February 1989

PAINTING IN RENAISSANCE SIENNA 1420–1500
Metropolitan Museum of Art, 82nd Street and Fifth Avenue, New York 21 December 1988–19 March 1989

ITALIAN ART IN THE 20TH CENTURY
Royal Academy of Arts, Piccadilly, London W1 14 January–9 April 1989

LEONARDO: ARTIST, SCIENTIST, INVENTOR
Hayward Gallery, South Bank, London SE1 26 January–18 April 1989

MIRO
Whitechapel Gallery, Whitechapel High Street, London E1 3 February–23 April 1989

ROYAL TREASURES OF SWEDEN 1550–1700
Royal Academy of Arts, Piccadilly, London W1 17 March–18 June 1989

100 Years of Russian Art Barbican Art Centre, Silk Street, London E1 27 April–9 July 1989

GAUGUIN
Grand Palais, Paris 14 January–20 April 1989 National Gallery of Art, Washington DC 1 May–31 July 1989

GOYA AND THE SPIRIT OF ENLIGHTENMENT
Metropolitan Museum of Art, 82nd Street and Fifth Avenue, New York 4 May–16 July 1989

LATIN-AMERICAN ART
Hayward Gallery, South Bank, London SE1 18 May–7 August 1989

DESIGN CALENDAR

Books of the Year

STEPHEN LONG

*I*n a year which brought sad news of the alteration of the
interiors and the ruination of the settings of several of Sir
Edwin Lutyens' houses, it is a pleasure to report that there
is one which remains absolutely intact. This little masterpiece
and its contents have been hardly touched by time since com-
pletion in 1924. The garden is just as Miss Jekyll planted it –
indeed her hoe and wheelbarrow are on the terrace. This happy
state of affairs was celebrated by May Stewart-Wilson in *Queen
Mary's Dolls' House* and cleverly photographed by David Cripps.
The house is not only a miracle of craftsmanship, but has now
become an invaluable record of Lutyens' ideal of upper class life
in the mid Twenties. Few books can have given such unalloyed
pleasure in 1988 as this one.

Three important books had notable new editions. Two of
these – *The Decorative Twenties* and *The Decorative Thirties* by
Martin Battersby, long out of print – have been lovingly revised
with scholarly care by Philippe Garner. He also contributes an
excellent short biography of Battersby to the first volume. The
other new edition is of Sir John Summerson's *Georgian London*. This
wonderful book has been almost completely re-written. In 1945,
it was one of the milestones along the road to acceptance and
then appreciation of Georgian architecture and a brilliant new

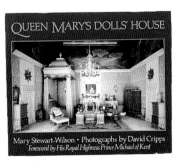

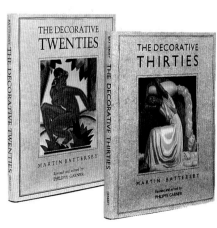

chapter has been added setting out these changes in attitude over the years. There are masses of new illustrations, many in colour.

A weekly perusal of *Country Life* is an exquisitely civilized pleasure enjoyed by everybody from the Queen downwards. Although the magazine has been given an unbecoming slick appearance lately, it keeps up its standards well. John Cornforth is a pillar of *Country Life* and has produced in *The Search for a Style* a survey of the magazine's attitude to interiors from its foundation by Edward Hudson in 1897 up to the mid-Thirties. It is a tantalising glimpse into what are now the rare bound volumes and tells us by what lengths so high a standard of photography was attained. For instance a view of the Entrance Hall at Heveningham with the marble floor, apparently highly polished, was achieved by photographing it wet. Even so, the feat must have meant many maids with many mops standing by! Cornforth contributes a perceptive commentary celebrating the noble past. Never avant-garde, *Country Life* nevertheless showed excellent modern interiors by Lutyens, Amyas Connell, Oliver Hill and so on. That many of the rooms look cheerless to us is mostly due to the tendency of the photographers (if the owners or, more probably, the house-keeper would let them) to push upholstered pieces and personal possessions out of range. Cornforth leaves off before the re-discovery of Victorian comfort.

Potentially the most important book on decorating in 1988 was the eagerly awaited *Twentieth-century Decoration* by Stephen Calloway. It was certainly the weightiest. The style, however, was light in a quite witty sub-Osbert Lancaster vein. It is hailed as a sequel to Peter Thornton's nastily titled *Authentic Decor*, although it overlaps it by a decade. It also carries on from where the incomparable Mario Praz retired exhausted. The book turns out to be a somewhat rag-bag and indigestible compilation of all Calloway has picked up in the course of his job as Keeper of Prints and Drawings at the Victoria and Albert Museum, and also from the series of lectures he commissioned on decorators of the past and by decorators of the present. Knowing readers will spot a few unexpected new plums among the disappointingly familiar illustrations. It was a formidable task to tackle and Calloway has produced – as indeed did Mario Praz – a thoroughly biased and personal anthology which is never dull, but leaves out almost as much as it has crammed in. It will by no means become the standard work on the subject, but high marks for trying and even for value in spite of the rather steep price.

The catalogue of the twin eye-opening exhibitions of the work of *George Bullock: Cabinet Maker* shared between Liverpool and London was one of the year's important and truly pioneering books. There is something thrilling when a glamorous new star is born or, in this case, re-discovered along with an almost unknown house such as Great Tew so largely furnished by him. The excitement spills over into this model catalogue which contains a sheaf of brilliant monographs on aspects of the master's work. Bullock was still only in his thirties when he died, but he

excelled at an astonishing range of skills from miniature wax portraits to the fitting up of a modest, but elegant pre-fabricated palace for the exiled Napoleon. Had Bullock lived longer he would surely have found a niche alongside Thomas Chippendale Sr. in that immortal pantheon of English cabinet-makers of whom everyone has heard.

There were an amazing number of books in 1988 on stencilling and other paint techniques. You can teach yourself dragging, stippling, marbling ad infinitum. Those eager to tell you how to do it are not content with walls and ceilings, but now cover every available surface, even the floor. Unless you are naturally talented in this field, choose the book with the simplest instructions for any hope of successful results.

Most people try to find inspiration in the rooms of others – often strangers to them – which they see in the pages of magazines. These, too, have proliferated and all have confusingly similar titles, appearance and, it must be confessed, contents. Two that stand out are our dear old pioneering war-horse *House and Garden*, which is better than ever, and the more recent *World of Interiors*. Min Hogg, editor of the latter, has produced *A Decoration Book*. To save us the trouble of ploughing through piles of dusty back-numbers, she gives a summary of the various themes she has relentlessly pursued. She groups interiors under headings: Minimal, Shabby-chic, Eccentric and so on. It is an excellent survey of the last decade and will be a help to tyros in choosing the way they might wish to go.

There were also many books on style, both at home and abroad, although David Hicks amazingly did not rush into print in 1988! One book that stands out is Mary Henderson's *Rooms*, telling us all about John Stefanidis. This is a beautifully produced affair and, after reading it, I feel it looks as if Mr Stefanidis is going to be the front runner in the Nineties – at least judging by the competition so far. He has long been famous for his beautiful and appropriate fitting out of Mediterranean villas; less well known are the rooms he has designed for the rigours of colder shores. Here is luxury, clean line, good colour, well-designed detail, in short: style. It is interesting to note how Stefanidis' sharp eye has gathered good ideas from past – and even present – masters and incorporated them into an ensemble uniquely his own.

Among the plethora of omnibus books gathering together motley selections of rooms under only vaguely appropriate titles, I enjoyed enormously *In An Irish House*, edited by Sybil Connolly. The well-known Connolly charm has inveigled owners to write about their houses and in most cases to include some delicious-sounding recipes too! She has even persuaded Molly Keane to contribute an amusing preface. There is something refreshingly unbuttoned about Irish interiors and they are much less self-conscious and fad-ridden than English or American ones. Even world-famous decorators mercifully seem a little affected by the prevailing *dolce far niente*. There is not much in this book of the

forlorn scenes of Ascendancy hanging on, seen in most books on Irish houses, and no stuffing pouring out of sofas. There is almost no melancholy, although it is sad to have a valedictory glimpse of the saloon at Birr Castle, still with its magnificent suite of furniture in situ. Happily the suite is still in Ireland and in as beautiful a setting. Leixlip in spite of certain deprivations looks as brilliant as ever, if not more so. I have perhaps a slight criticism of the Professor's photographs which do not capture the genius of the place in all cases: for instance, his view of the staircase at Dunsany does not do justice to one of the most magical architectural spaces in Ireland.

Finally, *Interior Visions*, a book about a habit until recently peculiar to the United States. These 'visions' are rooms in show – or as they are called in America, *show-case* houses and, with a few exceptions, a really rum lot they are too. Visitors pay a hefty fee to charity for admission – heftier still for the endless black-tie previews. Each room in the house is by a different designer all clamouring to catch the bored visitor or journalist's eye. Every decorative cliché and folly, every eye-catching device is brought into play. The most favoured style at present is still a mad and totally unlikely version of the English Country House Look. If you think it has been overdone here, peruse this book. Even Hollywood in its heyday was no madder and certainly more practical. The designers go berserk with yards and yards of no doubt charitably donated stuffs, they cram whole gardens of flowers into minute rooms and then stuff them with recklessly unrelated objects to create a spurious lived-in look. The bathrooms and bedrooms are remarkable indeed. For laughs, this book is a bit pricey perhaps, but it is a salutary lesson on How *Not* to Decorate.

QUEEN MARY'S DOLLS' HOUSE
Mary Stewart-Wilson with photographs by David Cripps
The Bodley Head   £15.00

THE DECORATIVE TWENTIES and THE DECORATIVE THIRTIES
Martin Battersby, revised and edited by Philippe Garner
The Herbert Press   £19.95

GEORGIAN LONDON
John Summerson
Barrie and Jenkins   £19.95

THE SEARCH FOR A STYLE: COUNTRY LIFE AND ARCHITECTURE 1897–1935
John Cornforth
Andre Deutsch/Country Life   £19.95

TWENTIETH-CENTURY DECORATION
Stephen Calloway
Weidenfeld & Nicolson   £50.00

GEORGE BULLOCK: CABINET MAKER
Various authors
John Murray/H. Blairman & Sons   £20.00

THE WORLD OF INTERIORS: A DECORATION BOOK
Min Hogg and Wendy Harrop
Conran Octopus   £25.00

ROOMS: DESIGN AND DECORATION
John Stefanidis and Mary Henderson
Weidenfeld & Nicolson   £30.00

IN AN IRISH HOUSE
Sybil Connolly
Weidenfeld & Nicolson   £16.95

INTERIOR VISIONS
Chris Casson Madden
Booth-Clibborn Editions   £28.00

Design Directory

LEADING SUPPLIERS TO THE BRITISH INTERIOR DESIGN INDUSTRY

Fabrics and Wallcoverings

Osborne & Little plc

FABRIC AND WALLPAPER DESIGNERS

A wealth of imaginative pattern and colour over a very broad spectrum characterizes Osborne & Little. Their distinctive, original approach has made them one of England's leading names in fine fabrics and wall papers and has brought them several design accolades, including the twice awarded British Design Award.

Pictured here is glorious mix of six of their new 1989 collections. Together they total 126 wallpapers, 50 borders, 40 trimmings and 115 fabrics including document chintzes, contemporary prints, tapestries and English woven silks.

Inspiration comes from an enormous variety of sources. For, rather than be locked into any one look, the design studio is interested in all aspects of design and continuously explores a wide range of styles suited to both the classic and the contemporary interior.

Interesting colourings are also sought and each collection introduces unusual shades, contrasts and combinations to add new dimensions even to the most classic document print.

For further information, please contact any of the following showrooms:

304–308 King's Road, London
SW3 5UH Tel: 01–352 1456
Fax: 01–673 8254

39 Queen Street, Edinburgh
EH2 3NH Tel: 031–225 5068

Barton Arcade, Deansgate,
Manchester M3 2AZ
Tel: 061–834 0475

Suite 1503N, 979 Third
Avenue, New York NY 10022
Tel: (212) 751 3333

Colefax and Fowler

INTERIOR DESIGNERS

Colefax and Fowler has long enjoyed a distinguished reputation for creating the English Country House style, an essentially simple and romantic style combining elegance and comfort.

In partnership first with Sybil Colefax in the 1930s and then with Nancy Lancaster, John Fowler had a notable influence on the development of interior decorating in the twentieth century.

Although the company's design reputation still rests with its interior decorators who carry out private and contract commissions worldwide, Colefax and Fowler has also become renowned for its traditional designs on chintzes, woven fabrics and wallpapers. Over the years the range of products has expanded to include painted furniture, upholstery, lighting and carpets. In addition to these is a range of accessories made exclusively for Colefax and

Fowler, which includes needlepoint cushions, hearth rugs, wool throws, a selection of room fragrances, pot-pourri and bathroom accessories.

Colefax and Fowler has showrooms in Mayfair, Chelsea and Belgravia. The original Brook Street premises provides a luxurious setting for antiques and includes a showroom for wallpapers, fabrics and trimmings. It is here that the decorating teams are based. The Fulham Road showroom, with its spacious interior, provides a perfect setting for the new range of accessories and gift items which have been intro-

duced to complement Colefax and Fowler's fabrics and wallpapers. An interior decorating service is also available from Fulham Road, and at all showrooms practical advice is available on colour schemes, curtain treatments and upholstery.

For further information, please contact our showrooms at:

39 Brook Street, London W1
Tel: 01–493 2231

110 Fulham road, London SW3 Tel: 01–244 7427

149 Ebury Street, London SW1
Tel: 01–730 9847

Manuel Canovas

FABRIC DESIGNS

'There are no ugly colours', says Manuel Canovas, 'there are only unfortunate combinations'. Manuel Canovas creates harmonies with colour in much the same manner as a composer creating symphonies with notes. Exercising the precision of a draughtsman and the highly sophisticated eye of a colourist, tones are used to strike sympathetic and ever-changing chords which occasionally surprise but never jar.

Inspired by his travels in Asia, India, North America and Europe, Manuel Canovas has been designing since the 1960s. In spite of the size of his far-flung empire, he continues to see himself primarily as an artist, spending hours in his studio on the rue Sedillot, Paris, drawing, mixing his palette and creating the intricately drawn and boldly coloured designs for which he is now world famous.

Manuel Canovas is not only a great traveller, but a great collector. Natural objects – pebbles, flowers, sands – surround him in his studio, providing artistic inspiration for colour, pattern, texture and shape. A painting picked up at an auction, a print glimpsed in a museum or catalogue, a colour seen in India without European equivalent, all are absorbed, incorporated, re-worked: a petal becomes larger, a painted vase subtly bluer. Since the creation of Les Tissues Manuel Canovas in 1963,

Photo: Monique Le Luthandre Stylist: Sarah Charles

Manuel Canovas has designed over 215 fabrics using flowers as a theme. In the 'Candides' collection, iris, peonies, tulips and field flowers, drawn with passion and precision, radiate the spontaneity of nature. In his jacquard designs, an intimate technical knowledge of weaving techniques allows the subtle opposition of yarns and colours, resulting in fabrics of a timeless authenticity and beauty.

Whether designing with stripes or checks, or mastering the art of an eighteenth-century *toile*, Manuel Canovas shows an informed respect for the patterns of the past, preserving their spirit even when colours or proportions are altered. From long forgotten patterns, themes are re-born and become part again of our daily lives.

For further information, please contact Manuel Canovas at:

2 North Terrace, Brompton Road,
London SW3 2BA
Tel: 01–225 2298
Fax: 01–823 7848

H A Percheron Ltd

FURNISHING FABRICS AND TRIMMINGS

Percheron was founded in London in 1898 by a Frenchman, Henri Arthur Percheron, in order to present the finest French furnishing textiles to British buyers. The company continued to be run by the Percheron family until 1983, when it was bought by three of its suppliers and Charles Hamer, who now runs the company as Managing Director.

Percheron are exclusive UK distributors of fine French and Italian fabrics by such famous Houses as Rubelli, Lauer, Edmond Petit, J Brochier Chotard, Tassinari & Chatel, Hamot, Burger and Veraseta. They also carry a wide range of trimmings and tie-backs from Reymondon.

As always, Percheron's fabrics, tie-backs and trimmings for 1989 reflect the quality and diversity of their suppliers. The new collections include velvets, prints, tapestries and *toiles* in colours ranging from delicate pastels to

deep rich jewel shades.

'Fleuraison' by Chotard is a collection of three co-ordinating cotton prints, featuring bold pink carnations on a background of small grey-blue flowers.

A dramatic linen print from Lauer, 'Nohant', combines fruits and flowers in a basket with interlinked garlands of flowers and leaves to form an impression of rich autumnal abundance.

Chotard's sumptuous cut velvet, 'Vertigo', depicts huge full-blown roses in shimmering colour, while 'Pils d'Ange' by Petit combines fringing and embroidery in pastel shades to produce an effect at once delicate and opulent.

Rubelli have introduced a plain cotton/silk moiré, 'Baudelaire', in thirty-four stunning colourways, and a range of lampas and brocades, many of

them on coloured grounds.

Percheron have extended their standard range of bullions, cords, etc. from Reymondon to include a matching tassel tie-back in sixty-four colourways. Their almost infinite range of custom-made tie-backs and trimmings continues to expand, and now includes an ornate chandelier hanger, as seen at Decorex 1988.

Percheron's extensive collection of fine European fabrics and trimmings is available through interior decorators and designers.

For further information, please contact H A Percheron Ltd at:

97–99 Cleveland Street,
London W1P 5PN
Tel: 01–580 5156 Telex: 22741
Fax: 01–631 4720

David Hicks International

FABRIC DESIGNERS

The Stratford Weaves Collection is the second in a series of annual collections designed by David Hicks for Tissage de Gravigny and Casal. The theme of geometric and floral motifs from the first collection, La Première, has been extended and elaborated, and has developed, as in the case of 'Orlando' and 'Lysander', into figurative designs almost like medieval tapestry.

The Collection is made up of six designs – 'Lysander', 'Cymbeline', 'Orlando', 'Oberon', 'Dorcas' and 'Touchstone' – in five colourways: gold/red/aubergine (see illustration); baby blue/oatmeal/apricot; dusty pink/sage green/baby blue/oatmeal; emerald green/raspberry/oatmeal; and royal blue/black/aubergine.

Conceived by David Hicks and developed in the Hicks design studio, this collection has been inspired by Japanese motifs, Portuguese arabesques and early English patterns.

'Britain, like most European countries, has always had an immense fascination for foreign art form, and being an extremely inquisitive designer I enjoy the excitement of travelling with my sketchbook and responding to new exotic influences, colours and flavours', says David Hicks.

The fabric composition is a mixture of cotton and fibranne and is suitable for upholstery. Prices range from £40.00 to £77.50 per metre (recommended retail price).

Also launched this year are the Jacquard St James Collection, Florence Wool and Yachting Cottons.

The Jacquard St James Collection is made of 100 per cent combed cotton, and consists of four designs – 'Battersea Dogtooth', 'Soho Stripe', 'Piccadilly Diamond' and 'Billingsgate Herringbone' – each in eleven colourways. This collection is suitable for upholstery and curtains and is priced at £26.50 per metre (recommended retail price).

Florence Wool tweed and Yachting Cotton are available in forty-two colours, and are suitable for upholstery and curtains. Florence Wool is priced at £23.00 per metre whilst Yachting Cotton is £12.50 per metre (recommended retail price).

All David Hicks collections are available through interior decorators.

For further information, please contact David Hicks International at:

4a Barley Mow Passage, Chiswick, London W4 4PH
Tel: 01–994 9222

Laura Ashley Decorator Collection

FABRIC AND WALLCOVERING DESIGNS

From the early days and throughout the growth of Laura Ashley Ltd, a great deal of attention was given to Bernard and Laura Ashley's homes around the world. These beautifully decorated houses demonstrated what could be achieved with a professional touch, now available to clients who require individual attention. From these beginnings a range of exclusively designed fabrics and wallcoverings with their own identity has developed into today's Decorator Collection.

A considerable amount of time is spent researching into the past, investigating various periods of history and the influence that colour and style has had upon interior design. Inspiration is drawn from all over the world, whether it be from documents, old fabrics, botanical prints or etchings and, as in the days of the Grand Tour, it is a way of recapturing the traditional English Country House look – a collector's way of decorating with the designs representing mementos from around the world.

This look that is so evident throughout the Decorator Collection offers endless combinations of design and colour, giving great versatility to the decorator and a continuing feeling of comfort and elegance, reminiscent of a bygone era.

The Laura Ashley design team are constantly researching for new collections. Recent launches in addition to our

cotton chintz and satin fabrics include 'Madras', a range of finely woven, pure cotton muslins consisting of six exclusive designs which reflect the unique traditional qualities of production that are associated with this fabric.

Especially for upholstery use, Laura Ashley has introduced 'Wovens', floral jacquard woven cotton designs in colours that harmonize with the palette of the collection.

The Decorator Collection is available through specialist retail outlets and interior designers, as well as our showrooms in Oxford, Edinburgh and London.

Illustrations: *above* 'Auricula Stripe' and 'Limelight' designs on cotton satin from the Brodick Castle Collection.

For further information, please contact our showrooms at:

71 Lower Sloane Street, London SW1W 8DA
Tel: 01–730 1771/4632

137 George Street, Edinburgh EH2 4JY Tel: 031–220 1961

26 Little Clarendon Street, Oxford OX1 2HU
Tel: 0865–52477

Warner Fabrics plc

FURNISHING FABRICS AND WALLCOVERINGS

Founded in 1870, Warner is one of the world's leading suppliers of quality products for furnishing and interior decoration, with an international reputation for design, colour and quality. The total range contains many thousands of printed and woven fabrics, in all design styles, and also a wide selection of related wallpapers. The aim is to offer an extensive choice for *any* interior theme.

Warner's range is designed in London by a large and highly skilled team, complemented by the ranges of Greeff Fabrics which are designed in New York. Many designs are based on archive material, and Warner's Archive is world-famous for its collection of historic fabrics and documents. In printed fabrics Warner are particularly known for their huge selection of traditional floral glazed chintzes. However, they also offer a very large range of other themes, including a wide choice of transitional and modern designs. As well as glazed chintz, cloths include high quality cottons, satins and linen unions. The comprehensive woven range includes damasks, tapestries, velvets, moirés, brocatelles, flat weaves, Madras nets and Nottingham lace, together with a large selection of plain weaves in many different textures and colours. Hand-woven silks can still be supplied to special order.

In wallpaper, Warner offer an ever-increasing number of pattern books to accompany many of the fabric designs.

Warner's London showroom displays the complete range of fabrics and wallpaper, and both trade and public are welcome to make use of its facilities. The showroom staff pride themselves on their friendly, helpful service.

Warner products are available throughout the world from interior decorators, department stores and leading local retailers, all of whom can rapidly obtain samples of any design they do not have in stock.

Please contact Warner's customer service department for further information at:

7–11 Noel Street, London
W1V 4AL Tel: 01–439 2411
Telex: 268317
Fax: 01–437 2608

The Design Archives

SPECIALIST FABRIC WHOLESALERS

The Design Archives opened its London showroom in September 1987 as a specialist wholesaler of eighteenth- and nineteenth-century furnishing fabrics, drawn from the superb collection owned by the Courtaulds Textile Group. This represents one of the largest and most exclusive archives of French and English designs to remain in private ownership in Europe at the present time.

The Design Archives' prints are produced in silk, cotton and linen union, and include a high proportion of traditional designs used by the best interior decorators in both the British and American markets.

1989 will see the launch of both woven and dyed upholstery weaves, some thirty new printed cotton and chintz designs and the first Wallpaper Collection.

For further information, please contact our showroom at:

79 Walton Street, London SW3
Tel: 01–581 3968

Watts of Westminster

HISTORIC FABRICS AND WALLPAPERS

restoration work by The National Trust, in the Houses of Parliament, the Colleges of Oxford and Cambridge and the gentlemen's clubs of Pall Mall, Watts' textiles and papers may also be found in the more modest houses of private

Watts & Co. is the living link with the splendours of eighteenth- and nineteenth-century decoration. Founded in 1874, the company was the creation of three eminent architects: Bodley, Scott and Garner. Their aim was to provide, according to an early advertisement, 'Embroidery, Textiles and Wallpaper', and thus ensuring complete artistic control over the interior decoration of their buildings.

Silk damasks, tapestries, woven stuffs, printed linens, period wallcoverings, all adhering to the designs established by the founders, are still in production. Extensively used in

clients. These are the most original and distinctive designs of their time, rivalled only by the work of Morris & Co.

Although the principle inspiration for the collection was drawn from the ethereal beauty of the late Gothic art of Northern Europe, the founders were responsible for initiating an archive that is probably the most comprehensive and accessible source of eighteenth- and nineteenth-century period designs in England.

For further information, please contact Watts & Co. at: 7 Tufton Street, Westminster, London SW1P 3QE
Tel: 01–222 2893

St Leger

DESIGNERS AND SUPPLIERS OF FABRICS AND FURNITURE

January 1989 saw the opening of St Leger's showroom at Chelsea Harbour. Colourful prints from our own collections are available in various 100 per cent cotton finishes, all retailing at under £20.00 per metre and stocked in London. Large-scale designs from Lino Gris add to the range.

Textural weaves from Esteban Figuerola reinforce this colour story and work well with the boldly designed prints. Eye-catching Anta plaids and stripes update the classic tartan – to order in silk, cotton or wool.

You will also find St Leger's own range of upholstery, plus Empire-inspired furniture. Its contemporary lines look well with their other collections, as do elegant lamps and co-ordinated trimmings.

A limited selection has been used by Rory Ramsden Ltd for their stand at the British Interior Design Exhibition 1989.

For further information, please contact St Leger at:

15 Garden Market, Chelsea Harbour, London SW10
Tel: 01–736 4370
Telex: 265871
Fax: 01–736 5698

Photo: Simon Wheeler, reproduced by kind permission of The World of Interiors

Zoffany Ltd

FABRIC AND WALLPAPER MANUFACTURERS

'Reveillon' is one of the designs taken from the Zoffany Archive Folio Collection.

The Archive Folio is a prestigious collection of several printed wallpapers reproduced faithfully from the originals in their own archive, and manufactured in their own factory. These designs can be obtained in their original colours as well as in various re-colours. The papers range in date from the middle of the seventeenth century to the mid-nineteenth century. 'Reveillon' itself dates from *c.* 1785–8, and is attributed to the French Reveillon factory. The design of arabesques with foliage and birds

is typical of the neo-classical style of pre-revolutionary France.

All Zoffany wallpapers and fabrics are taken from original documents. There is a large selection of machine-printed wallpapers and borders, and also cotton chintz fabric.

Zoffany products are available from most leading interior designers, and enquiries are welcome at our London showroom:

63 South Audley Street, London W1Y 5BF
Tel: 01–626 9262/01–493 7256
Telex: 291120 SOFLTD G
Fax: 01–493 7257

Furniture

David Linley Furniture

FURNITURE DESIGN

David Linley Furniture was established in 1985 and the original promise of providing top quality commissioned furniture remains the aim and objective of the company. They work closely with the client on each commission to ensure that the item meets the exacting house standards. A water-colour is prepared after the initial client consultation, and working drawings are completed in London and approved by the client. Different projects are then undertaken by a team of highly trained craftsmen who specialize in techniques that are now rather rare – marquetry, parquetry and cabinet-making.

David Linley Furniture's work this year illustrates the versatility and flexibility of the company. As well as their private commissions, they have, for example, designed and executed a total refit for the jeweller Theo Fennell in his Fulham Road showroom, and have completed a special large display cabinet for the interior

decorators Beckett & Graham in their shop off the Kings Road.

David Linley Furniture have also built an original cabinet for the Dulwich Picture Gallery, which stands in the Linley Gallery. The design of the cabinet bears the hallmark of David Linley, but also reflects the architecture of the

gallery. The style of Sir John Soane is apparent in the cabinet, especially Soane's shallow domed shapes, which are worked into the marquetry design. The ornamentation also refers to Soane's sar-cophagi shapes on the gallery's exterior, as the Dulwich Picture Gallery houses the benefactor's mausoleum.

Whether designing for the Metropolitan Museum of Art in New York or for private commissions, David Linley Furniture always produces furniture that is beautiful and of the very best quality.

For further information please contact the David Linley Furniture showroom at:

1 New Kings Road, London SW6 4SB Tel: 01–736 6886

The Dining Room Shop

ANTIQUES, FURNITURE, CHINA AND GLASS

The Dining Room Shop is the only one of its kind in Britain. Specializing in everything to do with the table, the shop has a large and varied stock of antique tables, chairs and other dining-room furniture, as well as china, glass, table linen, candlesticks, prints of eating and drinking and other small accessories. While about 75 per cent of the stock is antique, the rest is modern or reproduction.

You can have a china dinner service specially designed, or choose from a wide selection of made-to-order reproduction and modern dining chairs and tables. These range from rustic French-style cherry tables, made to any size in four weeks, to sophisticated circular mahogany tables, gilded and carved with fine inlays, and fully upholstered dining chairs.

Directors' dining rooms are also furnished, from sideboards to table napkins, and the shop runs a specialized antique-finding service for private customers and decorators.

For further information, please contact The Dining Room Shop at:
62/64 White Hart Lane, London SW13 0PZ
Tel: 01–878 1020

Carew-Jones & Associates Ltd

CUSTOM-MADE FURNITURE AND INTERIOR DECORATION

The Carew-Jones & Associates' showroom is a joint venture between Nigel Carew-Jones and a small number of specialist British contemporary furniture manufacturers. The aim of the showroom is to have one central location where interior designers and architects can see representative pieces of furniture from these specialist workshops. Most of the furniture is custom-made to the client's own requirements, and finishes include lacquer, metal, perspex and upholstery.

The showroom is strictly for designers and architects only and aims to promote the use of British-made furniture to the

designer market.

For further information, please contact Carew-Jones & Associates Ltd at:

188 Walton Street, London SW3 2JL Tel: 01–225 2411

Nicholas Dyson Furniture Ltd

FURNITURE DESIGNERS AND MANUFACTURERS

Nicholas Dyson Furniture Ltd design and make furniture of high quality and distinctive appearance to meet the individual requirements of private, business and institutional clients.

As well as working to direct commission from private individuals and corporate bodies, they also collaborate with architects, interior designers and other professional specifiers, to whom they offer design, prototyping or manufacturing services tailored to particular needs.

Much of their work consists of individual items, but they also have the capacity and experience to handle substantial batches and sets of fur-

niture. Their versatility as designers, and the exceptional array of skills available in their workshop and from their associated suppliers, enable them to undertake a very wide range of projects and furniture types. Their capabilities are appropriate wherever there is a requirement for high quality, purpose-made furniture. The scope of their work reflects the varied commissions they receive.

For further information, please contact Nicholas Dyson or Aled Lewis at:
Unit 2, Home Farm,
Ardington, Wantage,
Oxfordshire, OX12 8PN
Tel: 0235–834311
Fax: 0235–833072

Derek Frost Associates Ltd

Unique furniture to commission.

Illustration: Scarf console table. Burr maple and satinwood veneers combine with two-tone white gold gilding inlaid with mother-of-pearl squares. Overall size: 180 cm × 52 cm × 20 cm/ 70 in × $20\frac{1}{2}$ in × $7\frac{1}{2}$ in.

For further information, please contact Derek Frost Associates Ltd at:

Moreton Yard,
Moreton Terrace Mews North,
London SW1V 2NT
Tel: 01–828 6270

Inventive Design Ltd

FURNITURE BY NICK ALLEN

From the rich detail of his classically inspired satinwood veneered desks to the skeletal forms of his sophisticated Studio Collection – a range of metal furniture with wooden or glass surfaces – Nick Allen's designs are both practical and elegant.

Produced in a variety of styles, the furniture reflects many ethnic and classical influences. Pieces can be entirely original commissions or may draw on previous orders.

Inventive Design ensures that the same meticulous attention is given to each item, carefully controlling the production costs with agreed budgets on design and manufacture.

Commissions have included an architectural desk derived from Palladian designs to dining tables with polychromatic decorative finishes. The Victoria and Albert Museum in London has recently purchased a stool from the versatile steel-framed Studio Range for display.

Inventive Design also offers a consultancy service working in conjunction with architects and interior designers on furniture design content.

Illustration: bronze dressing mirror. Cast by the lost wax and sand cast processes, the frame is made in bronze and

given a weathered verdigris patina. The glass is hand bevelled. The mirror is finished all round, the back being inlaid. Diameter 33 cm × width 50 cm × height 42 cm.

For further information, please contact Inventive Design Ltd at: 156 Ifield Road, London SW10 9AF
Tel: 01–373 2216

Peter Dudgeon

ENGLISH SOFAMAKERS

For over forty years Peter Dudgeon have been making elegant English sofas and armchairs using traditional methods and materials. Their showroom, which displays over thirty standard designs, has been on the same site between Harrods and Beauchamp Place since 1947. William Dudgeon, son of founder Peter Dudgeon, with twenty-five years upholstery experience and partner Hugh Garforth-Bles, with over seven years furniture experience, have concentrated recently on improving both the quality of personal service and updating the designs and comfort of their sofas.

Dudgeons' furniture is made in their own workshops using, as always, the best traditional skills and ingredients. No foam is used. There are four critical elements: dowelled beech frames; individual double cone springs tied by hand in both the seat and upholstered back; horsehair and natural fibre applied by hand; and natural cane lashed onto the front springs of the seat platform. All are labour-intensive skilled processes. The cane edge is the only proper method of giving a soft yet resilient sprung seat edge. All sofas have hand-sewn finishing.

Thirty-six standard designs are available encompassing the best of English styles; all proportions may be varied, if required. The company is committed to launching new collections each spring and autumn. Three were launched in March 1989: a deep, divided upholstered-back model; a camelback sofa with mahogany stretcher; and a P-armed style with 100 per cent pure down back and seat.

Peter Dudgeon re-cover and re-upholster quality antique furniture. They also make one-off designs to customers' own specifications or to match existing pieces; nothing is too complex. An exclusive thirty-five model range of traditional leather sofas and chairs is marketed, which uses the best traditional construction and hand-coloured, antiqued rawhide. During 1989 a small collection of genuine French chairs will be launched.

1988 was the company's most successful year in its history. Customers have included several Royal families, ambassadors' residences have been furnished both here and abroad, together with many others where quality and traditional values are important. Peter Dudgeon is proud to uphold the best traditions of sofamaking and continues to create elegant examples of understated English taste.

For further information, please contact Peter Dudgeon at:
Brompton Place, Knightsbridge, London SW3 1QE
Tel: 01-589 0322

Lawson Kelly

DESIGNERS OF SOFAS AND ARMCHAIRS

Lawson Kelly have been making traditionally built sofas and armchairs since the war. Only natural materials are used on hardwood frames with hand-sprung seats and backs amongst other upholstery techniques.

As each piece is made to order, and constructed to last a considerable period of time, there is no restriction on the length of a sofa, or more importantly, the depth. All dimensions are alterable and all design features are interchangeable.

A selection of designs is on display in the workshop, to be viewed by appointment.

For further information, please contact Lawson Kelly at: Unit 4, Heliport Industrial Estate, 40 Lomard Road, London SW11
Tel: 01–228 9812

Sudeley Design Ltd

INTERIOR DESIGNERS

Sudeley Castle Furniture is characterized by fine classical design that is practical for modern-day living, for both home and contract use. Inspired by original pieces still in place at Sudeley Castle, this furniture is handmade and hand-finished.

The occasional furniture is available immediately from stock. Finishes are carefully chosen to integrate with any interior as would an antique. The much acclaimed four-poster beds are available on short delivery even though finished to specification. Special commissions can be discussed.

The Jermyn Street show flat also has an interesting collection of upholstery, antiques and accessories, making it a useful address for busy designers.

For further information, please contact Nicola Nelson at:

The Penthouse, 130 Jermyn Street, London SW1Y 4UL
Tel: 01–828 8200

Sudeley Design Ltd, Sudeley Castle, Winchcombe, Cheltenham GL54 5JD
Tel: 0242 602 308

George Smith Ltd

FABRIC AND FURNISHINGS SUPPLIERS

George Smith Ltd are manufacturers of traditionally designed handmade furnishings and suppliers of fabrics from major English, French and Italian fabric houses including the full Bennison fabric range. They also stock an extensive range of sofas, chairs and other accessories. Their company has operated successfully for several years and has acquired an enviable reputation supplying retail and trade customers, nationally and internationally.

Standards are second to none with the accent being on finesse and quality. Every piece carries substantial guarantees and can be made to suit the architectural requirements of most interiors. Only the best materials are used (they do not use foam). Well-seasoned beechwood is used for the frames, giving strength, rigidity and durability. Heavy jute webbing is used to support steel coil springs which are hand-sewn into position in both the seat and back. The springs are covered with 10 oz (284 g) hessian, then layered with horsehair. A covering of 8 oz (227 g) hessian is applied, after which all contours are hand-sewn throughout. Layers of horsehair are added and the whole piece is covered with cotton calico. Finally, a thick layer of cotton wadding is applied and the customer's choice of fabric is hand-sewn into place, as are valances and skirts, if required. All cushions are duck-down filled; legs are hand polished and only solid brass castors are fitted. The final result is a magnificent piece of George Smith furniture.

For further information, please contact George Smith Ltd at:

587–589 Kings Road, London SW6 Tel: 01–384 1004 Fax: 01–731 4451

48 Old Market Street, Bristol BS2 0EX Tel: 0272–556417/ 554939 Fax: 0272–554997

Antiques and
Decorative Prints

Bennison

FINE ART DEALERS AND INTERIOR DESIGNERS

Bennison specialize in eighteenth- and nineteenth-century antiques of interest to interior designers and decorators, with whom they deal extensively on both sides of the Atlantic, and members of the public interested in finding exactly the right pieces for a particular room setting.

The firm carries a large and imaginative stock of furniture, as well as making their own useful range of 'antique' light fittings, including the Bennison standing lamp, which is both understated and an attractive alternative to predictable lighting. They also make a popular and competitively priced range of scroll-backed dining-room chairs, copied from an eighteenth-century design, which can be covered in horsehair or other fabrics of your choice. Other items made by Bennison's own team of specialized craftsmen include coffee tables, wall bracket lamps, and plaster busts for libraries, studies and conservatories, and joinery work from large bookcases to bedside cabinets.

Bennison was founded over twenty years ago by Geoffrey Bennison, probably the most charismatic and influential decorator in England until his untimely death in 1984. Now owned and managed by Bennison's former assistant Christopher Hodsoll, fresh ideas and interpretations have been introduced to the Pimlico-based business, while the high standards of design and attention to detail set by its founder have been maintained.

For further information, please contact Bennison at:

91 Pimlico Road,
London SW1W 8PH
Tel: 01–730 3370/8076
Fax: 01–730 1516

Mallett at Bourdon House

FINE ART DEALERS

Bourdon House in the heart of Mayfair, until 1953 the London house of the late 2nd Duke of Westminster, has an interesting history. Built for William Bourdon Esq. in the years 1723–5, during the reign of George I, the house stood amidst fields and market-gardens between the then emerging developments of Berkeley Square and Hanover Square.

The property came into the family of the future Dukes of Westminster through the marriage in 1677 of Sir Thomas Grosvenor to Miss Mary Davies (hence Davies Street), the beautiful daughter of a local yeoman. Some fifty years later, this land was leased to the Burdons, who shortly afterwards started to build a house there.

Bourdon House has retained its connection with the Grosvenor family for nearly three centuries and is still a property of their estate; today it remains substantially unchanged.

Within this charming period setting there are a number of rooms filled with fascinating French and Continental furniture of the eighteenth and nineteenth centuries, objets d'art, decorative pictures, bibelots and amusing accessories. The furniture stock is more eclectic than that at the shop in Bond Street; it includes rare and important masterpieces together with exotic lesser items and other pieces of

eccentric interest. The general taste is unique in combining unusual charm with quality of design and craftsmanship.

There is also a small attractive paved courtyard which provides the perfect background for antique garden statuary, ornaments and fur-

niture, another exclusive feature of the business.

For further information, please contact Mallett at: 2 Davies Street, Berkeley Square, London W1Y 1LJ
Tel: 01–629 2444
Telex: 25692
Fax: 01–495 3179

Christie's

FINE ART AUCTIONEERS

There is no better source of new ideas for interior design than an auction house like Christie's, which specializes in antiques from every period.

Each year Christie's holds hundreds of auctions of interest to the interior designer, covering everything from furniture, carpets and paintings to porcelain, glass and china. The range and quality of the items to be sold is probably unequalled by any other single source. For example, the contents of the flat of celebrated interior designer Geoffrey Bennison were sold at Christie's (see illustrations: *below* The Drawing Room at 4 Audley Square, London W1; *bottom* Geoffrey Bennison's flat re-created in Christie's Great Rooms for viewing prior to the sale).

Catalogues are published well in advance of the sales and each one contains numerous photographs together with detailed information about the provenance, size, materials used and estimated price.

When you find items of interest, come and see them at the pre-sale viewing and discuss them with members of the specialist departments concerned. Should you decide to bid, you can either attend the sale or leave a written bid with us.

Many clients find it more convenient to take out an annual subscription, which ensures that you receive all relevant catalogues automatically.

To help you select the right catalogue subscriptions we have recently published a brochure which gives details of the large variety of categories of sales at Christie's, together with the prices for each. There is also a useful brochure, *Buying and Selling at Christie's*, which is freely available.

We look forward to welcoming you to any of our sale-rooms listed below, or at any of our regional offices. Please ring 01–839 9060 for further details.

8 King Street, St James's, London SW1
85 Old Brompton Road, London SW7
164/166 Bath Street, Glasgow G2

O'Shea Gallery

SPECIALIST DEALERS IN ANTIQUE PRINTS AND MAPS

The O'Shea Gallery specializes in prints and maps from the fifteenth to the nineteenth century. Their stock of maps, charts and scenic views covers all parts of the world and is viewed by county, country and continent.

Their extensive collection of prints includes topographical and decorative subjects, natural history, and sporting and marine scenes, and offers one of the largest selections of prints in the United Kingdom. Shown here is a print of tulips from Johann Weinmann's *Phytanthoza Iconographia*, published in Germany, 1737–1745.

The O'Shea Gallery is represented in New York by Kensington Place Antiques, and throughout the United States by Baker Knapp and Tubbs showrooms in Atlanta, Boston, Chicago, Cleveland, Dallas, Washington, Dania, Los Angeles, Laguna Niguel, Minneapoiis, Philadelphia, San Francisco and Troy.

They issue catalogues and hold regular gallery exhibitions, as well as exhibiting at fairs. In 1989, UK fairs will include the Chelsea Antiques Fair (14–25 March); the British Interior Design Exhibition (25 May–18 June); Olympia Fine Art and Antiques Fair (9–18 June); Grosvenor House (14–24 June); Chelsea Antiques Fair (13–24 September); The Northern Antiques Fair (28 September–4 October); Park Lane Hotel Antiques Fair (2–8 October); Burlington House Antiques Fair (3–11 November).

A full framing service is available to interior designers, decorators and collectors. The range includes handpainted, stippled, marblised, and decorated mounts and frames as well as traditional silk and wash line mounts and French gold leaf frames.

For further information, please contact the O'Shea Gallery at:
89 Lower Sloane Street,
London SW1W 8DA
Tel: 01-730 0081/2

Lucy B Campbell

FINE ART PRINTS

The Lucy B Campbell Gallery is situated in Holland Park Avenue, London W11. It specializes in prints from the seventeenth to the nineteenth century, and also presents the work of a select group of contemporary artists. Lucy B Campbell's Gallery represents the most affordable collection of fine art now available to collectors, decorators and investors.

Lucy B Campbell has been collecting prints for many years, and as her expertise has grown, so has her collection of fine prints. She now has over 6,000 prints in stock and the range of subject is wider than can be found anywhere else in London – birds, fruit, fish, animals, interiors and architecture, all of the highest

quality. Prices range from £20.00 to thousands of pounds, depending on the rarity of the print. However, the quality remains the same.

The Lucy B Campbell Gallery also offers an excellent framing service of individually designed, handmade mounts and frames, and offers worldwide shipping facilities. Lucy B Campbell instructs her own framers in choosing the mounts and frames for her prints; or, if customers wish to choose their own mounts, she will use her experience and intuitive judgment to advise them.

Lucy B Campbell also has representatives in New York and Toronto where the showrooms are open to clients by appointment only.

For further information, please contact:

Lucy B Campbell, 80 Holland Park Avenue, London W11 3RE Tel: 01–229 4252

Judy Cormier, 164 East 72nd Street, New York NY 10021 Tel: (212) 517 3993

Barbara Kingstone, 188 Balmoral Avenue, Toronto, Ontario M4V 1J6 Tel: (416) 967 3930

ANAS PENELOPE, Mas.

Specialist Decorative Finishes

Francesca Di Blasi

SPECIALIST WALL FINISHES

Francesca Di Blasi is now introducing in London extraordinary wall finishes and centuries-old techniques translated into modern interiors. Finishes with impeccable pedigrees and beautiful names: Stucco Lustro Veneziano, Encaustic Stucco, Marmorina, Limewash and true Fresco.

A profound love for the classic traditions of her native Italy, coupled with the realization that painted imitations could never quite re-create the same effects and atmosphere, prompted a period of study and research into the reconstruction of original finishes. 'I took what can be described as "a voyage back into the past". Back to when beauty and perfection mattered more than the speed of execution.' Years of patient research in museums, in books, with old artisans, yielded a wealth of 'recipes', some with extraordinary ingredients: milk, soap, honey, rice water. 'We tried them all. Some turned out to be simply impractical, others surprisingly contemporary; the effects suited both traditional and ultra-modern decoration alike.'

Eventually, Colorificio Paulin of Feltre in Italy developed the perfect formula for a range of products perfectly balanced and strictly faithful to the original finishes. Only minor concessions to modernity were made by substituting lesser ingredients not suited to today's centrally heated interiors. 'They are stucco and lime-plaster finishes in a very serious vein, not a superficial coat of paint but physically part of the walls. They are dedicated to those who appreciate the difference and who have time for beauty.'

Shown here is an example of the Stucco Lustro Veneziano finish called 'Doge', which gives an incredibly smooth, polished surface effect.
For further information, please contact Francesca Di Blasi at:

P.O. Box 506, London SW1W 0LY
Tel: 01-730 6401

Photo: Gerald Lopez

Antonia Spowers Designs

STENCIL DESIGNER

Stencil designer and decorative artist, Antonia Spowers specializes in interpretative design of any period for the decoration of walls, floors and textiles.

A seventeenth-century Persian Kerman carpet was the inspiration for this stencilled floor at Dorney Court, near Windsor. Flowers, trees, birds and hunting animals are enclosed in a lattice pattern and over thirty stencils build up a rich texture.

Antonia Spowers also markets her own collection of stencil kits which can be used to create decorative effects on a variety of surfaces from old plaster to rich velvet.

Commissions are undertaken for exclusive designs and exotic rooms both in Britain and abroad.

For catalogues and commissions, please contact

Antonia Spowers at:

Unit 3, Ransome's Dock, 35/37 Parkgate Road, London SW11 4NP Tel: 01–622 3636 Fax: 01–228 2118

Pimlico Print Rooms

PRINT ROOM DESIGNERS

Pimlico Print Rooms are recognized as the leading designers of traditional eighteenth-century style Print Rooms. Using original methods of design and construction, the prints are pasted directly onto the walls and bordered, linked and embellished by chains, ribbons, ropes, trophies and masks all cut from paper sheets.

The company holds an extensive stock of antique decorative prints on a variety of subjects ranging from architectural and botanical motifs to sporting and topographic scenes. Shown here is a corner of a Print Room utilizing eighteenth-century views of Kew Gardens and Roman antiquities. Recent commissions include boardrooms, dining rooms, bathrooms and studies both in Europe and America.

Pimlico Print Rooms also supply prints in period frames and create print screens, large decorative boxes and panels, all of which can be finished in traditional paint finishes. Also available is a range of friezes and false dado rails, including a Gothic collection.

For further information, please contact Pierre Spake, tel: 01–978 1103 or Pimlico Print Rooms, tel: 01–821 1577

DESIGN DIRECTORY

Roderick Booth-Jones

MURALS

Roderick Booth-Jones brings to his work a skill as a draughtsman that would be hard to match; an approach to a subject which constantly intrigues; a fascination with materials which finds him equally at home with canvas or concrete; an enthusiasm for his medium which leaves both artist and client satisfied.

The understanding he has for murals leaves him open to any kind of commission: the smallest arch or the largest atrium, a single small panel or the entire cavernous mass of a huge vaulted building.

Illustrations:
above Private swimming pool, acrylic on concrete, 42 feet long × 24 feet wide × 9 feet high/12·8 m × 7·3 m × 2·7 m.
left Anamorphic garden in a Chelsea dining room, 29 feet long × 5 feet high/8·8 m × 1·5 m

For further information, please contact:

Roderick Booth-Jones
14 Davisville Road, London
W12 Tel: 01–740 6781

DESIGN DIRECTORY

135

Statuary, Garden Ornament and Garden Design

Seago

PERIOD GARDEN ORNAMENT AND STATUARY

Timothy and Lindy Seago, with their new garden gallery, have brought to London's Pimlico Road something bright, fresh and very different. The shop is not only new but quite unique in as much as it is the only place in London specializing solely in exterior design and the supply of garden ornaments and statuary.

In designing the interior of the shop, Tim and Lindy's intention was to re-create the peace, solitude and beauty of a classical garden to play host to their fine range of stock. Wall murals by the renowned English artist Gilly Szego create a backdrop for a massive nineteenth-century terracotta vase decorated with windswept faces and entwined serpent handles. Classical columns and impressive dentil mouldings surround a profusely carved nineteenth-century marble seat with two satyrs sitting lazily at either end, and elegant but simple entrance gates beckon you towards a Temple of Apollo where the god's lifesize marble effigy stands overlooking a deeply carved chalk vase with profuse fruiting vine decoration.

As well as the sale of statuary directly from their shop, the Seagos also run another unique service – Exterior Design. Not to be confused with landscape architecture, this consultancy service involves their viewing gardens and estates in order to advise on the type, size and location of

garden ornamentation and then the supply of the same. The design element they bring to their business is something they consider of paramount importance.

'Designing is like painting. In our case we take a palette of

vases, statues, fountains and sundials to complete a picture. A well-placed and well-chosen bird-bath will complete a town garden just as much as the inclusion of lifesize statuary in a country estate.'

To date their design service has dressed such diverse areas as a 140-foot balcony in Knightsbridge overlooking Hyde Park; conservatories in Harrogate and Richmond; a country estate in Buckinghamshire and a 10-foot square garden in East Sheen.

Something different? Certainly!

For further information, please contact Seago at: 22 Pimlico Road, London SW1W 8LJ Tel: 01–730 7502 Fax: 01–730 9179

Clifton Little Venice

GARDEN FURNITURE AND WORKS OF ART

Gardens are as subject to fashion as any other art form. For years they have been adorned with statues and architectural features, although by the eighteenth century the old traditions of Renaissance craftmanship had become less important than the natural landscape. The reign of Queen Victoria saw horticulture as the dominant theme in the English garden and new techniques led to mass produced ornaments, so that every villa soon had a cast-iron urn or pottery edging tiles. Today, discerning gardeners are once again looking for beautiful objects to complete their garden pictures. There is a new respect for old skills, while improved methods of restoration have rescued many garden ornaments from neglect and decay.

Clifton Little Venice specializes in original works of art for the garden and conservatory. Fountains, follies, urns and statues in stone, marble, lead and iron, all form part of the changing collection of objects from our heritage. There are seats in wood and iron, as well as period gates and benches of stone or plinths in marcasite or similar exotic materials. The pieces range in size from 20-foot columns to 2-inch hand-turned flower pots and the shop offers a personal service for those in search of the unusual; particular pieces are often found for both interiors and gardens.

Original garden furniture is increasingly scarce and often expensive, but in an effort to supply objects of quality at a reasonable cost, Clifton Little Venice has recently begun to copy a limited range of chairs and wirework, with a strong emphasis on good design and original craftsmanship.

Clifton Little Venice can be found just off the Regent's Canal and next door to Clifton Nurseries. This exceptional garden centre sells a wide selection of plants for gardens and interior landscapes. Mature trees and shrubs and handsome topiary are features at the nursery, which provides an ideal background for displaying garden ornaments.

For further information, please contact Clifton Little Venice at:
3 Warwick Place, London W9
Tel: 01–289 7894

Crowther of Syon Lodge

INTERIOR AND EXTERIOR ARCHITECTURAL DEALERS

Four generations of buying and selling have made Crowther of Syon Lodge Britain's longest established interior and exterior architectural dealers. The wealth of knowledge accumulated through the years has ensured the expert acquisition of the market's finest pieces. Each piece is a major architectural landmark, specially selected for its ability to enhance and transform its environment – a quality which can be fully appreciated in the unique and tranquil setting of Syon Lodge.

Shown here are *right* a fine mid-nineteenth century marble figure of Diana at the Bath by John Warrington Wood (1839–1886), which is signed 'J. Warrington Wood. Roma'; and *right* a nineteenth-century marble chimneypiece supported by lion monopodia jambs, the frieze centred by a keystone in the form of a lion's mask.

For a copy of our brochure, please contact:

Jerrard Nares,
Crowther of Syon Lodge,
Busch Corner, London Road,
Isleworth, Middlesex
TW7 5BH
Tel: 01–560 7978
Telex: 8951308 SYONUK G
Fax: 01–568 7572

Inchbald School of Design

COURSES IN ALL ASPECTS OF DESIGN

The Inchbald School of Design, renowned worldwide for its progressive approach to the teaching of design, will be celebrating thirty years in design education in 1990.

The Inchbald School's curriculum covers courses varying in length from five days to three years, with a broad spectrum of design subjects, both practical and theoretical. The Environmental Design course leads the way with a three-year training in all aspects of exterior and interior design. Two-year Master Diploma and one-year Diploma courses are run in Environmental Design, Interior Design, Garden Design and the History of Architecture & Design.

The one-year Garden Design course is limited to fifteen students. Training in the

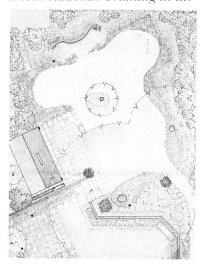

principles of design, in plant knowledge, manipulation and exploitation in design, and in garden architecture and landscapes, is combined with projects which include formal gardens, leisure complexes and urban landscaping.

Inchbald training paves the way to a wide variety of professional careers in the field of design and all its related areas.

Illustration: Design for a Residential Garden by P. Wichtl, Dip.ISD (1988).

Brochures available from the Inchbald School of Design at:
32 Eccleston Square, London SW1V Tel: 01–630 9011/2/3

The Chelsea Gardener

PLANTS AND GARDEN DESIGN

The Chelsea Gardener is the only place in central London where designers can find rare and exotic indoor and outdoor plants of mature size, as well as everything for the London garden including topiary, terracotta, urns, statues, *treillage* and even temples, bridges and gazebos. Top quality garden furniture is a speciality throughout the year.

The Bookshop has over 1,000 titles on gardening, garden design, garden history and conservatories, as well as reprints of garden classics and a second-hand department.

The Chelsea Gardener is the source of imaginative

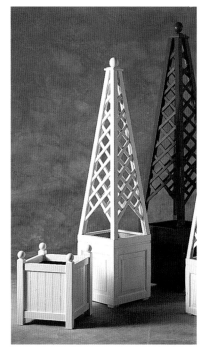

plants and gardens. If they have not got a particular variety, they may have it at their larger branch at Crews Hill, north London. Otherwise they will always try to find it for you.

They are open seven days a week throughout the year.

For further information, please contact The Chelsea Gardener at:

125 Sydney Street, Kings Road, London SW3 6NR
Tel: 01–352 5656

Crews Hill, Enfield Heath, London EN2 9DP
Tel: 01–367 9323

Siddeley Landscapes

INTERIOR AND EXTERIOR LANDSCAPE DESIGNERS

Historically, garden design has always been a part of English culture, although people generally seem to associate it with stately homes, country mansions and palaces. Now, however, landscaping has grown into an easily available industry offering a virtually unlimited variety of services to all. It also provides a range of design solutions from instant and attractive surroundings for large commercial developments through to the transformation of the most ordinary garden, patio or roof terrace into an extension of the home.

Siddeley Landscapes, working in conjunction with their landscape architect, a property developer or private client, specialize in designing and constructing exterior landscapes tailor-made to compliment the building and its surroundings. A water feature can be integrated into a courtyard where the light restrictions are unsympathetic to the requirements of most vegetation; roof terraces and patios can be enhanced with an imaginative combination of

trelliswork, paving or decking, and containerized or built-in planting schemes. Specimen plants, mature at planting, are used to give a 'finished' effect and colour schemes are carefully chosen to provide continual colour and interest throughout the year. Existing features can be integrated into the overall design. Working to a budgeted cost, Siddeley Landscapes use every square foot or acre to its full potential, resulting in a functional, attractive and easily maintained design.

The term garden design is not, of course, restricted to exterior landscaping only. For instance, again using innovative designs, themes and planting schemes, the interior landscape of a home, office, shop or shopping centre can be made to override any limitations of light and space, and the impact of special features and focal points enhanced.

Siddeley Landscapes, with their wide-ranging services, will continue to meet the growing demand for imaginative landscaping schemes and are proud to belong to an industry that has become an integral part of modern living.

For further information, please contact Siddeley Landscapes Ltd at:
1/11 Chelsea Garden Market, Chelsea Habour, London SW10 0XF
Tel: 01–351 2010
Fax: 01–351 3095

Specialist Joinery

Finecraft Ltd

ARCHITECTURAL JOINERY AND SPECIALIST DECORATION

Finecraft has been established for thirty years as a leading contractor for high quality commercial and domestic interiors, architectural joinery and specialist decoration. The company maintains a highly qualified team of tradesmen and specialists for all requirements from electrical and plumbing installations to decoration. Contracts have been undertaken across a broad spectrum of design styles ranging from traditional to the latest in high tech. Shown here is a design for a Chairman's Office, created for the British

Interior Design Exhibition 1988.

Finecraft enjoys a reputation for high quality joinery, including kitchens, bedroom units, bookcases and doors. This work can be carried out to specification, or to designs prepared by their team in consultation with the client.

The company has worked extensively with leading interior designers and architects, and takes pride in completing jobs to schedule and to the highest standard. Contracts have been successfully completed for leading design-

ers such as Gordon Lindsay; Christopher Nevile Partnership; Terence Dinsdale; Peter Stern and Seabrooke Alexander. Other commissions include Maxim's Casino; Next Plc; Park House, Richmond; Coombe Hill Golf Club and the new headquarters for the Hulton Picture Company. For further information, please contact Finecraft Ltd at:

Arundel House, Arundel Road, Uxbridge, Middlesex
UB8 2RX
Tel: 0895 72244/33101

Ashley Stocks Ltd

CABINET-MAKERS

Ashley Stocks are specialists in the manufacture of made-to-measure furniture and associated products, combining traditional skills with modern machining methods to produce furniture of the highest possible quality. Furniture, both traditional and modern, is designed, planned and installed to individual requirements.

The Ashley range of free-standing furniture (see the tallboy *right*) includes sofa tables, sideboards, bedside cupboards and dressing tables. Small-batch runs allow the production of custom-made pieces from this range to individual sizes.

Specialist manufactured furniture includes complete fitted bedroom units, bureaux, bookcases and chests-of-drawers. Illustrated (*below*) is a family room unit in white ash incorporating a kitchenette.

Apart from supplying private customers, Ashley Stocks are happy to work with other designers, producing quality one-off pieces for office interiors, reception areas and executive suites.

For more information and a colour brochure, please contact Ashley Stocks Ltd at:

Units 9 and 10, Parkfield Industrial Estate, Culvert Place, London SW11 5BA
Tel: 01–627 1222
Fax: 01–622 1053

Becher Joinery Ltd

JOINERS, CABINET-MAKERS AND FURNITURE DESIGNERS

Oak, Ash, Cherry, Cabinets, Windows, M.D.F., Shop Fronts, Meranti, Turning, Sycamore, Shop Interiors, Mortise, Elm, Body Shops, Plywood, Lathes, English Heritage, Plane Tree, Mosque, Design, Finishing, Afrormosia, Lroko, Spindle, Routers, Teak, Veneering, Crosscut, Beech, Brazilian, Maple, Ramin, Jelutong, Keruing, Rosewood, Cedar, Gaboon, Birch, Zebrano, Cellulose, Wenge, Padauk. We make it in wood. We design and make. We make to your design.

For further information, please contact Becher Joinery Ltd at:

Unit 1, Church Wharf, Corney Road, London W4 2RA
Tel: 01-994 0889 Fax: 01-994 0697

Inigo Designs Ltd

CABINET-MAKING, JOINERY, ANTIQUE RESTORATION

Inigo Designs are specialist cabinet-makers and architectural joiners, able to meet the most exacting demands of both corporate and private clients.

They are able to produce custom-made furniture in a traditional style, although over the last eight years their main expertise has been working to contemporary designs in modern environments. In this respect, Inigo Designs make a valuable contribution towards the integration of wood as a feature in overall design requirements.

For further information, please contact Inigo Designs at:

Downside Works, Highway Farm, Downside, Cobham, Surrey KT11 3JZ
Tel: 0932 67862

Commercial Interiors

Gordon Lindsay
INTERIOR DESIGN

Meeting the brief; reflecting the personality of the client, projecting the Corporate or individual image. All are part of the designer's task: together with high quality materials and workmanship. This is the policy of Gordon Lindsay and his friendly, efficient partnership.

For further information please contact Gordon Lindsay at:
The Gatehouse,
2 Devonhurst Place,
Heathfield Terrace,
London W4 4JD
Tel: 01-994 9988

Rory Ramsden at Blase Designs Limited

INTERIOR DESIGN AND DECORATION

Rory Ramsden will design your office, reception area, meeting rooms or your complete suite of management offices. They work independently or as part of your professional team. They offer a complete turnkey service, from initial concept sketches through to relocation management.

They have completed projects for banks, advertising agencies, commercial organizations and accounting practices, all to exacting standards.

Attention to detail is paramount from the client's initial brief to work study analysis, space planning, budgeting, programming, project man-agement and finally to corporate identity proposals and implementation.

Through their building division, they offer a complete installation service including air conditioning, lighting, heating, custom-made joinery and specialist finishes.

Corporate offices need to reflect the dynamics of their occupiers and their relative position in the market place. Great care is taken to create a tailor-made environment that achieves this, as well as being an intrinsically satisfying place to conduct business.

For more information, please contact Rory Ramsden at:

11 Osiers Road,
London SW18 1NL
Tel: 01-877 0626
Fax: 01-877 0676

Helen Cooper Associates

INTERIOR DESIGN AND DECORATION

Photo: Rory Carnegie Photography

The power of decoration is an understated influence.

Imagine the unconscious per-suasion of space; the confidence of colour; the definition of light; and the statement of function. Rooms create moods. Ideally a space creates a background for its characters like a stage for its cast, and on entering a mood is set and its influence begins to work.

The Chairman's office is a haven, created for comfort and congeniality, and exuding an unspoken comprehension of command and confidence. Tinged with warmth, it cap-tures the icons of a career, while providing individuality, which is irreplaceable. (Ack-nowledgements to Christopher Hodsoll, Rice Paper, Belinda Coote and IQR.)

For further information, please contact:

Helen Cooper Associates Ltd,
53 St Martin's Lane,
London WC2
Tel: 01-240 0711
Fax: 01-240 6697

Baroness Ilona Ludwig,
Helen Cooper Associates (USA),
316 West 90th Street,
New York NY 10024
Tel: (212) 874 0925
Fax: (212) 689 4964

David Hicks International

COMMERCIAL INTERIOR DESIGNERS

An interior by David Hicks International (DHI) combines efficiency with aesthetics and forms a timeless statement of corporate quality.

The 'Hicks' look is unmistakable, using strong classical architectural detailing, often with wood and stone finishes; bold and yet subtle colour, pattern and texture mixes; and custom-made furniture. It is tailored and uncluttered, and above all, infinitely practical.

DHI creates interiors for hotels, restaurants, clubs, shops, offices, yachts, show houses and more. For example, the Ciel Bleu Cocktail Bar and Restaurant in the Okura Hotel, Amsterdam (*top right*), was designed by DHI. The cocktail bar is screened from the restaurant by diamond-cut and acid-etched glass in Art Nouveau style. Tub chairs are covered in textured weave with contrast red piping with stained oak wood frames. The walls are panelled in stained oak as well with mirrored banding, and the floor is covered with a Hicks Brussels weave carpet design.

DHI was also commissioned to design a reception area and desk for Citibank in The Savoy Buildings, London (*below right*). The walls, pilaster columns and desk top are of granite; maple wood with ebonised banding was used to panel the desk itself; and again, the 'Hicks' Brussels weave carpet with border was used to cover the floor.

With interior, architectural, graphic and product designers as well as project managers and craftsmen, the company has the ability and technical skills to undertake almost any kind of project.

The company has the added advantage of David Hicks Associates in Paris, Rome, Athens, Tokyo and Sydney. In Australia, DHI has formed an interior design partnership with a leading architectural practice.

A design-and-build or turnkey service is available anywhere in the world.

DHI commissions often involve more specific tasks, and its designers frequently create for clients new fabrics and carpet designs, purpose-built furniture, lighting and signage.

Whatever the budget, DHI design expertise and knowledge of sourcing will ensure the best quality finish available within the financial constraints of the project.

For further information, please contact David Hicks International at:

4a Barley Mow Passage, Chiswick, London W4 4PH
Tel: 01-994 9222

Kitchens and Bathrooms

Blase Designs plc

INTERIOR DESIGNERS

Blase Designs plc are designers and makers of bespoke fitted and freestanding furniture for all parts of the home or office.

They offer a unique service for both private and professional clients, whereby anything is possible in any size, style, colour, material and finish; from hammerite kitchens to mahogany boardroom tables. This service is invaluable to the client who does not want to compromise.

All their furniture is manufactured in our own workshops and their clients are invited to see their own work being produced at any stage of its manufacture.

They are flexible in that they can produce and install a kitchen to a client's specification just as easily as the design and co-ordination of a complete office refurbishment and all that it entails. Full interior design, building works, lighting, electrical and plumbing details, tiles and tiling, decoration, fitted and freestanding

furniture, soft furnishings and curtains, all these aspects can be covered in conjunction with their sister companies, Blase

Developments Ltd and Rory Ramsden at Blase Designs Ltd.

Their main aim is to create furniture and environments that are individual yet practical, of the very highest quality materials and workmanship, and above all exactly what the client wants.

If you require any further details on their products or services, or would like to discuss a particular project with their design team, please contact Blase Designs plc at:

11 Osiers Road, London SW18
1NL Tel: 01–874 4421
Fax: 01–877 0676

Arena of Oxford

KITCHEN DESIGNERS

What makes an Arena kitchen work so well? There is a rightness about an Arena kitchen which is wonderfully pleasing in this day and age. It looks as though it has grown out of the home that it belongs in – and indeed, this is exactly the case. Except for appliances – ovens, sinks etc – nothing in an Arena kitchen is ready-made. Arena has no catalogues, no units, no preconceptions. The project will not even get under way until an Arena designer has visited your home and thoroughly understood the way you and your family live.

Everything takes shape around this concept. Plans, materials, surfaces, the pattern and size of tiles – in fact, the whole kitchen is conceived, designed and built for one client, one home, one lifestyle.

Determined to preserve and respect the ambience of the room illustrated *right*, they reproduced the detailing of its old pine china cupboard in open shelving and wall cupboards. Solid maple worktops with inset terracotta tiles abut the Aga, and old pine floor units are scribed to the flagstone floor.

Their show kitchens are on view at Thomas' Yard, Oxford.

For a colour brochure, please contact Arena at:

Thomas' Yard, Rectory Road, St Clements, Oxford OX4 1BP
Tel: 0865–726505

Crabtree Kitchens

KITCHEN DESIGNERS

Crabtree, established for over fifteen years, provide a complete kitchen service from initial discussion, through detailed design and manufacture, to installation of furniture and appliances. Crabtree's imaginative and personal approach is equally well suited to private clients, interior designers and developers. Projects completed recently include eighteen kitchens for two exclusive developments in Knightsbridge, as well as many individual commissions.

Crabtree manufacture exquisite kitchens, whether the brief is for post-modern, as shown here, or for high gloss and stainless steel, or for a traditional style in hardwood or with a hand-painted finish. Crabtree also produce dining-room furniture on a commission basis to complement their kitchen designs. Made to their customers' exact specifications, the tables and chairs are available in either natural or limed oak, natural or stained ash, maple, or with a hand-painted finish in simple classical styles.

Crabtree, by paying meticulous attention to detail, maximise the potential of any kitchen area, and interpret and develop ideas to create a unique, beautiful and practical kitchen. Crabtree's comprehensive service covers London and the surrounding area. For further information, please contact Crabtree Kitchens at: The Twickenham Centre, Norcutt Road, Twickenham TW2 6SR
Tel: 01-755 1121

H & C Creative

BESPOKE FURNISHING

H & C Creative is a business collaboration of artists, craftsmen and designers offering a one-off service. Any domestic, trade or industrial requirements for specialist high quality artefacts, furniture and installations can be fulfilled. Serving a large range of clients from building contractors, through furniture makers to the photographic and advertising world, H & C Creative are able to offer a complete service from conception to delivery and/or fitting of the product. A client can commission work from any stage in the creative process – design, architectural development, working drawings, prototyping, manufacturing, installation. Using a large pool of specialized services, and with designers and craftsmen working closely together, they are able to avoid the usual problems of both designer/makers and larger-scale manufacturers, suffering from neither limited facilities or skills, nor limited liaison or involvement in any given project. They provide a working umbrella organization with access to appropriate supporting services, and most important of all, they form a definite tie between all those involved in any project.

The core of the organization is a 7,500 square foot studio workshop in Battersea. At a location convenient to central London, there are comprehensive facilities for both wood and metalworking, spray

finishing and vitreous enamelling, in addition to which local services can be drawn on for requirements as wide as sheet metal forming, screen printing and upholstery. A large naturally lit studio provides 2,400 square feet of space ideal for setting out and pre-building larger work prior to installation and, coupled with the workshop, allows for pre-assembly of products such as bespoke kitchens at the point of manufacture, leading to fewer on-site complications.

The ability of H & C Creative to design and/or make furnishing and decorative objects out of virtually any materials has a wide variety of applications, and the broad base of skills offered, coupled with their aesthetic sensibilities, ensures that any project that is undertaken receives careful attention to detail and finish, as well as considered construction and effective turnround.

For further information, please contact H & C Creative at:
64–68 Stewarts Road,
London SW8 4DE
Tel: 01-720 0223

DESIGN DIRECTORY

Max Pike's Bathroom Shop

BATHROOM DESIGN

Max Pike has been creating bathrooms for a sophisticated clientèle for over six years, and is now known as the authoritative voice on bathroom design – sometimes unorthodox, always uncompromising.

In 1981 Max Pike's Bathroom Shop was established. The concept was to create a showroom for the best and most innovative of bathroom products, but at the same time a place where designers, clients and ideas would converge.

The Max Pike design ethos is simple – to reconcile aesthetics with the practical considerations of durability, functionalism and lasting design appeal. Steering clear of the kitsch and the clinical, Max Pike offers the perfect solution, and takes a personal interest in the individual requirements of every client.

If the quality and design is faultless, if it is the best of its kind on the market and matches Max Pike's exacting standards, then you will find it at his Bathroom Shop. A stunning range of baths, basins, lavatories and fittings are on display. At the top end of the market is the luxurious 'Kallista' range of baths in heavy gauge Armacryl. Stylishly simple and available in the colour of the client's specification, these baths are exclusive to Max Pike. For a more classical alternative, Max Pike's own 'Belgravia' range is an increasingly popular choice.

The simplest bath can be elegantly accessorized with beautiful taps from the 'Belgravia' range classical designs. More exotic is the range of taps and accessories by 'Kallista', exclusive to Max Pike. Designed in any metal, from gold to shiny nickel, they will disgorge your bath water via chutes, waterfalls or spouts.

Steam and hydramassage baths complete the picture. A recent addition to this hedonistic range is Max Pike's own Hydramassage system with discreet but powerful solid brass jets and controls plated to match any of the thirty ranges of taps currently on show.

Max Pike brings a wealth of experience and tremendous flair to the world of bathrooms. His ebullient personality and boundless enthusiasm when working alongside interior designers and architects is the necessary catalyst for any design project.

For further information, please contact Max Pike's Bathroom Shop at: 4 Eccleston Street, London SW1W 9LN Tel: 01–730 7216

Rugs and Carpets

David Black

ORIENTAL CARPETS

David Black has been in business at his gallery for twenty-five years and has established a respected position in the field of Oriental carpets. The gallery stocks a comprehensive range of tribal and village rugs, kilims, Scandinavian weavings, antique embroideries, decorative carpets and a fine selection of Indian dhurries. Prices range from £100 to £50,000. The gallery regularly mounts exhibitions devoted to various themes and aspects of the carpet world.

David Black was one of the first specialists to introduce collectors and interior designers to twentieth-century tribal rugs. In the last few years, fine kilims have been woven once again using traditional designs, handspun yarns and vibrant vegetable dyes. David Black appreciates that antique carpets now attain prices beyond the resources of many collectors and enthusiasts. These modern examples thus provide a decorative alternative as well as being collectors' items of the future.

David Black is happy to act as a consultant with regard to valuation and insurance. He frequently gives guidance on individual collections, both new and established, and will represent clients at auctions and other sales. He is accustomed to working with architects and interior designers, as well as with museums and collectors.

The gallery has its own restoration workshop which employs a team of experts familiar with the problems of rugs and carpets. A cleaning service is also available, and David Black will advise on condition, repair etc.

David Black is keen to draw attention to areas of rug-making which are not well-known, and to make them more accessible to collectors he has written and published numerous books, including *The Rugs of the Wandering Baluchi*, *The Undiscovered Kilim* and *Woven Gardens*. His most recent publication is *World Rugs and Carpets*, published by Country Life, which provides a comprehensive guide to the design, provenance and acquisition of carpets.

The gallery is conveniently situated near the Holland Park underground station, close to the West End – where the collector is met with informative guidance in a congenial atmosphere.

For further information, please contact David Black at: 96 Portland Road, London W11 4LN Tel: 01-727 2566

Afia Carpets

CUSTOM-MADE CARPETS AND RUGS

Afia Carpets, recently granted the Royal Warrant as carpet supplies to H.M. The Queen, have over seventy-five years experience in custom-made carpets and rugs. Each unique design is beautifully made in pure wool, patterned and coloured to reflect the themes of a room and its furnishings. Colour sketches are prepared within two weeks of visiting the showroom.

Custom-made pieces are made either by machine, on 27-inch Wilton looms, or by hand, woven to an exact size and shape – a highly glamorous look which can be even further enhanced by special effects such as carving and embossing.

Fine borders are one of Afia Carpets' hallmarks. Ranging from simple bands to highly decorative patterns, these can be used to splendid effect, creating staircase runners, defining landings and highlighting features such as fireplaces.

Afia also have a stock Wilton range called 'Georgetown', a neat pattern with fine loop pile, available in three colourways in broadloom width for immediate delivery.

For further information, please contact Afia Carpets at: 60 Baker Street, London W1 Tel: 01–935 0414 Fax: 01–486 6126

Roger Oates Design Associates

CUSTOM-MADE RUGS

Roger Oates Design Associates is a unique studio producing rugs, from custom-made designs to collections of both tufted and flat-woven rugs, all made in 100 per cent pure new wool.

Two tufted collections – 'Abstract' and 'Fragments' – won a British Design Award in 1988. The latest designs – 'Cloister' (illustrated) and 'Colonnade' – show a simplicity of line and proportion in strong architectural colours.

The flat-woven rugs are studio-woven by hand and range from pinstripe herringbone patterns to large and small chequerboards.

The designers, Fay Morgan and Roger Oates, are able to offer a very wide choice of colouring for the rugs which are often made-up in response to a brief from an architect or interior designer. Apart from the design, a particular appeal of these high quality rugs is the outstanding flexibility in both size and colour that Roger Oates Design Associates is able to offer.

For further information, please contact Roger Oates Design Associates at: Church Lane, Ledbury, Herefordshire HR8 1DW Tel: 0531 2718 Telex: 35827 HJ PG Fax: 0531 5570

Vigo Carpet Gallery

ANTIQUE AND REPRODUCTION CARPETS AND RUGS

There are those who have expressed surprise that a gallery so long associated with the best in antique rugs should be making such a name with its reproductions. The philosophy has not actually changed for at Vigo they have always been more concerned with the way a rug looks on the floor than the way it looks on paper. Age of itself is no virtue and most people, it is hoped, would rather have an attractive new rug with full pile but of unexalted name than an ugly antique design from a much acclaimed factory.

Vigo is aware, probably more than anyone else, just how difficult it has become to find a European rug which combines all the necessary elements of size, colour, condition, design and price to suit your specific needs.

Rather than compromise or forever pursue the impossible, you can now commission just the rug you want from the Vigo Carpet Gallery. The right size, the right design, the right

colour to match the curtains, and in any of the traditional European techniques: needlework, Aubusson or Savonnerie-style knotted carpets or Gobelin-technique tapestries.

There is also a very large stock of their own designs, most derived from antique pieces which have passed through the gallery at some time during this century. The carpet shown *left* was made by Vigo for His Grace the Duke of Beaufort at Badminton House.

For further information, please contact the Vigo Carpet Gallery at:
6A Vigo Street,
London W1X 1AH
Tel: 01-439 6971
Fax: 01-439 2353

Tiles

Paris Ceramics

TILE DESIGN AND RESTORATION

Paris Ceramics is not a 'shop' in the usual sense of the word a place where people can drop in when they happen to be passing by. The showroom is open by appointment only because owners Steve Charles and Clifford Jones feel that their tiles, in all their myriad forms, deserve both time and attention.

It is a small business, owned and run by experts, and offering a number of highly specialized services. These include restoring and matching antique tiles and a complete design and installation service, an important element of which is the production of full colour plans, showing the tiles as they will be seen in situ. Working with the ceramic artist Doug Watson, they undertake a great many 'one-off' commissions for painted tile murals and they supply and fit throughout Britain, Europe and the United States.

Paris Ceramics are probably best known for the antique terracotta and stone floors which they reclaim from French country houses. Every floor is quite different, reflecting the regional colour variations of the original clay and stone, and the tiles require skilled interpretation. Clifford Jones is almost certainly Britain's leading authority on the reclamation, restoration and re-laying of these antique floors.

Because the supply of old floors is so limited, they also work with a unique family firm

in Spain, which maintains an unbroken tradition of terracotta tile-making which stretches back to the arrival of the Moors in Spain.

These new floors have all the characteristic colours and textures of the old tiles, but are readily available in any quantity and can be distressed to give them an 'antique' finish. Amongst their other floors are 'Blue English Limestone' and a new range of unglazed decorated floor tiles; made from a very hardwearing composition stone material, they are available in a number of different designs, with matching borders and plain tiles which allow the build-up of ornate patterns.

Their wall tiles, from Holland, France and Spain, include numerous panels and

series, many of which depict historical themes, such as seventeenth-century Signs of the Zodiac. From the tile-makers in Spain they also commission a remarkable series of panels depicting figures from mediaeval life – from courtiers to tradesmen. Royal Makkum, Europe's oldest established ceramics factory, supplies them with a number of patterns, some of which date from the 1600s.

For an appointment to visit the showroom, please telephone 01–228 5785.

For a full colour brochure, please contact Paris Ceramics at:

543 Battersea Park Road, London SW11 3BL
Fax: 01–924 2282

Art Tiles

TILE DESIGNS

With their prestigious Victorian range, Art Tiles have endeavoured to recapture the vigour and panache that distinguished the most innovative years of the British tile industry.

The finest craftsmanship of that period can be seen in a range which offers a com-prehensive and extensively researched collection of tiles and mouldings.

A variety of finishes are available including the exquis-ite 'Majolica' hand- painted and decorated, pressed and embossed wall tiles.

Colour-matched to com-pliment the wall tile collection, Art Tiles' floor tile range has evolved from original nine-teenth-century encaustic designs.

For further information, please contact Art Tiles at:

Heathfield, Newton Abbot, Devon TQ12 6RF
Tel: 0626–832641

Candy Tiles

TILE DESIGNS

Candy Tiles has introduced a range of Victorian reproduction tiles that faithfully recreate the elegance and style of the Victorian age.

Traditionally made from high quality clays, you can choose from repeated pattern tiles, border patterns and delft motifs in a choice of rich colours ranging from peacock blue to olive green.

Influenced by the work of acclaimed Victorian designers William De Morgan and William Morris, the wide selection of classic designs evokes the true splendour of the age.

This range of Victorian tiles are right at the forefront of the current vogue for the co-ordination and mood of the Victorian look.

For further information, please contact Candy Tiles at:

Heathfield, Newton Abbot, Devon TQ12 6RF
Tel: 0626–832641

Fired Earth

TILE DESIGNS

Fired Earth is best known for a comprehensive range of terracotta floors, and in recent years their expertise in both new and reclaimed terracotta has become well established. Whilst continuing to develop existing products, the company is constantly extending its area of interest and is now able to offer a unique selection of beautiful floor and wall tiles.

Fired Earth has recently sourced extraordinary hand-riven slate tiles from quarries in China, India and Africa. With such evocative names as 'Tiger Pink', 'Sahara'. 'Bhutan Green', 'Mandalay' and 'Twilight' it is easy to see how other slates just look grey!

In response to the revival of interest in decorated and geometric floors, Fired Earth has launched a range of encaustic floor tiles. Hand-made in stoneware, and employing techniques first used over 1,000 years ago, these tiles are available at around the same price as many vinyl copies.

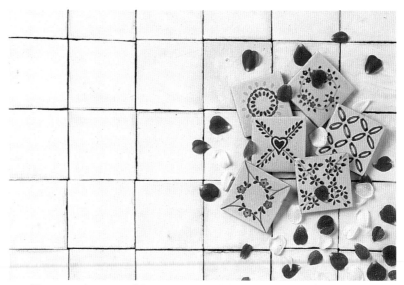

To complement this extensive range of floor tiles, Fired Earth also specializes in decorated wall tiles handmade by artisans from around the world.

In association with their atelier in Provence, the company is able to provide the interior designer with a vast palette of over 100 stunning colour glazes from the 'Haut Provence' range.

The success of Fired Earth's 'Early English Delft' has led the company to introduce a wider spectrum of original designs from workshops in Holland, Brazil and France.

This fascination with delftware has further led the company to acquire a unique collection of antique delft, recently auctioned at Christie's. These tiles are to form part of an historic tile library soon to be on display in the new Fired Earth showroom in Bath. A reproduction set of seventeenth-century Saracene tiles from this collection has been commissioned and will soon be available in a limited edition.

For a full colour brochure, packed with bright ideas, please contact Fired Earth at any of our showrooms:

37–41 Battersea High Street, London SW11 3JF
Tel: 01-924 2272

3 Saracen Street, Bath

Middle Aston, Oxfordshire OX5 3PX Tel: 0869 40724

Acknowledgements

The publishers would like to thank all individuals and organizations involved for their kind help in providing information and material for this book, as well as those who allowed their designs or interiors to be photographed.

Picture research Julia Brown.

The following credits for photographers and agencies, with all known architects and designers, are listed by page number.

2–3   Photo David Garcia/Design Zoffany Ltd (see also pp. 6, 8, 20, 36, 40, 46, 52, 60, 68, 72, 78, 88, 92, 100, 102, 106, 108, 118, 126, 132, 136, 142, 146, 152, 158, 160

8   Photo John Spragg/Design Richard Lowe

9   Above Photo Arabella Ashley/Design Simon Playle
        Below Photo Arabella Ashley/Design Joanna Trading

10   Photo Arabella Ashley/Design Parish-Hadley Inc

11   Photo Arabella Ashley/Design Alidad

12   Above Photo Arabella Ashley/Design Anna Tatham
        Below Photo Arabella Ashley/Design Jonathan Hudson

13   Left Photo Arabella Ashley/Design Sudeley Design
        Above Photo Arabella Ashley/Design Rossie Designs
        Below Photo Arabella Ashley/Design Ian Shaw

14   Above Photo Arabella Ashley/Design Blase Designs
        Below Photo Arabella Ashley/Design Rory Ramsden
        Right Photo Arabella Ashley/Design Beckett & Graham

15   Left Photo Arabella Ashley/Design Woodstock Designs with Spencer-Churchill Designs
        Above Photo Arabella Ashley/Design Indiaworks
        Below Photo Arabella Ashley/Design Gordon Lindsay

16   Photo Arabella Ashley/Design David Hicks International

17   Above Photo Arabella Ashley/Design Anthony Paine/Architects Wiltshier Interiors
        Below Photo Arabella Ashley/Design Bennison

18   Left and Above Photo Arabella Ashley/Design Mercier-London
        Below Photo Arabella Ashley/Design Norland Interiors

19   Photo Arabella Ashley/Design Parke Interiors with Machin Designs

20   Visual Sybil Anderson/Design Manuel Canovas

21   Photo John Spragg/Visual Geoff Barnard/Design David Hicks International

22   Above Photo Jeremy Whitaker/Visual Nicholas Glover/Design Nicholas Glover
        Below Visual Reg Trundle and Tony Coolley/Design Broosk Interior Designs

23   Above Visual Caroline Aitken/Design MC²
        Below Visual Rico Nanty/Design Mary Fox Linton

24   Visual Chris Constantinou/Design Rory Ramsden at Blase Designs

25   Above Visual Georges Andraos/Design Mercier-London
        Below Visual/Design Gavin Renwick and Jaqueline Smith for the Royal College of Art, London

26–7   Visual/Design Bonetti & Garouste

28   Above Visual/Design George Spencer
        Below Visual Denis Fullerton/Design Scarisbrick & Bate

29   Above Visual Catriona Terris/Design Robina Cayzer Ltd
        Below Visual Marianne Topham/Design Morrow Reis Designs

30   Visual Marianne Topham/Design Parke Interiors

31   Above Visual/Design Simon Playle
        Below Visual Marianne Topham/Design Beaudesert
        Right Visual Marianne Topham/Design Designers Guild

32   Left Visual Venetia Maynard/Design Alidad
        Right Visual Caroline Aitken/Design Ian Shaw

33   Visual Marianne Topham/Design Rosemary Hamilton

34   Visual Hugh Robson/Design Meltons Ltd

35   Visual Nicola Wingate-Saul/Design Pimlico Print Rooms

37   Photo courtesy *Country Life*/Design Tom Parr

38   Photo courtesy Colefax & Fowler/Design John Fowler

39   Photo courtesy Claremont Furnishing Fabrics Ltd

41   Photo/Design Mercier-London

42   Photo/Design Jameson Design Ltd

44   Photo Fritz von der Schulenburg/Design Stephane Boudin/Courtesy Leeds Castle

45   Photo courtesy Mary Fox Lindon/Design Pascal Mourgue

47   Photo/Design Danny Lane

49   Above Photo Etienne Bol/Design Fred Baier
        Below Photo John McCarthy/Design Sally Hampton
        Right Photo/Design Carol McNicoll

50   Above left Photo Patrick Shanahan/Design Joanna Short
        Above right Photo/Design Gordon Burnett
        Below left Photo/Design Sasha Ward
        Below right Photo/Design Tom Eisl

54   Photo courtesy Alan Powers

55   Above Photo/Architect Roderick Gradidge
        Below Photo Angelo Hornak

56–7   Photo/Architect Roderick Gradidge

58   Above and Below Photo courtesy *Country Life*/Architect Roderick Gradidge

59   Visual Anthony Ballantine/Architect Roderick Gradidge

61   Photo Richard Bryant (Arcaid)/Architect I M Pei

62   Photo Richard Bryant (Arcaid)/Architect Gae Aulenti

63   Photo Richard Bryant (Arcaid)/Architect Richard Rogers

Wrought-iron 'snail bench' designed by
Colin Chetwood.